SALVADOR & BAHIA

MICHAEL SOMMERS

Contents

Bahia

I t's the rare visitor who isn't mesmerized by São Salvador da Bahia dos Santos. With its flood of baroque churches in an idyllic setting overlooking the shimmering Bay of All Saints, Brazil's first capital is magical.

Bahians refers to it as *axé,* or "good energy." But the truth is that in Salvador, life flows in a different rhythm. Like the warm Atlantic waters that lap its shores, time is more liquid here. Its balmy climate, sea breezes, and enticing beaches are constant companions. Music, too, is everywhere—from the chants of the beach vendors hawking grilled shrimp to the twang of the one-string *berimbaus,* a bow-shaped instrument of African origin that accompanies spinning *capoeiristas* as they practice their graceful combination of dance and martial art. African elements seep into every facet of Bahian culture: from language and music to religion and food. Fused together with Catholic elements, this African legacy is vibrantly on display in the dozens of popular *festas* that invade the streets in the summer. Of course, Soteropolitanos (as the capital's inhabitants are known) are never hard-pressed to find an excuse for a party.

It would be a crime not to visit Bahia's capital city of Salvador, but it would be pure sin to miss the many natural, historic, and cultural attractions within the largest of Brazil's northeastern states: the gentle hills and decaying sugarcane plantations of the Recôncavo region that ring the Baía de Todos os Santos; the colonial towns of Santo Amaro and Cachoeira, both known for their religious celebrations; and a long string of idyllic beach towns stretching along the coast.

PLANNING YOUR TIME

For some travelers, Salvador is a complete destination in itself. Certainly the city offers a rich local culture, dazzling baroque architecture, a pulsing nightlife, relaxing beaches, and (in summer) some of the most colorful and popular *festas* in Brazil. To get a taste of the place, spend at least 3-4 days. Toss in the easily accessible surrounding area with its idyllic beaches, the colonial towns of the Reconcâvo region, the spectacular natural attractions of

Highlights

★ **Carnaval:** Billed by the *Guinness Book of World Records* as the world's biggest street party, Salvador's mind-blowing Carnaval is also Brazil's longest, lasting a full seven days (page 26).

★ **Mangue Seco:** On Bahia's northern coast, Mangue Seco is a deserted paradise of dunes, palms, rivers, and ocean (page 41).

★ **Cachoeira:** This sleepy colonial town on the banks of the Rio Paraguaçu preserves some of the African diaspora's oldest religious and musical traditions (page 43).

★ **Parque Nacional da Chapada Diamantina:** In the heart of Bahia's arid interior, this lush, mountainous plateau region is filled with hiking trails, waterfalls, and colonial diamond-mining towns (page 46).

★ **Barra Grande:** Perched on Brazil's third largest bay, the Baía de Camamu, Barra Grande boasts a laid-back vibe and stunning beaches, including the Taipu de Fora (page 58).

★ **Trancoso:** The ultimate in hippie chic, the village of Trancoso is cosmopolitan yet rustic, and blessed with stunning beaches (page 71).

★ **Pelourinho:** The winding streets of Salvador's colonial center are awash in museums, music, magnificent baroque churches, and faded treasures that conjure up its glory days as Brazil's first capital (page 8).

★ **Igreja e Convento de São Francisco and the Igreja da Ordem Terceira de São Francisco:** The adjoining church and convent devoted to St. Francis are some of the most glorious examples of baroque art in all Brazil (page 13).

★ **Caraíva:** For an idyllic, away-from-it-all beach experience, it's hard to beat the rustic charms of this tiny fishing village surrounded by some of Bahia's most gorgeous and deserted beaches (page 74).

★ **Parque Nacional Marinho dos Abrolhos:** This offshore marine reserve is a diver's delight; both Charles Darwin and Jacques Cousteau were impressed by the spectacle of sea life here (page 77).

Bahia

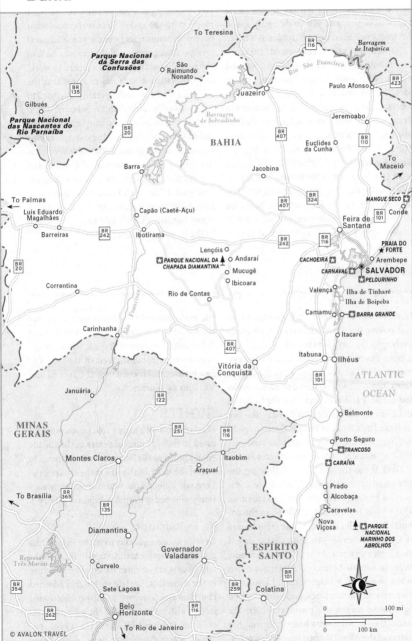

© AVALON TRAVEL

the Parque Nacional da Chapada Diamantina, and a pilgrimage to one or several of the famed beaches along Bahia's northern or southern coasts, and you could easily spend 2-3 weeks in Bahia, using Salvador as a base.

Bahia can be visited year-round. The summer months of December-March are the hottest, with temperatures hovering around 35°C (95°F) and lots of sun. This is high tourist season, as travelers from throughout Brazil and the world descend on many of the most popular coastal resorts (Praia do Forte, Morro de São Paulo, Itacaré, Porto Seguro, Arraial d'Ajuda, and Trancoso). The upside is an endless array of festivities. The downside is that prices usually rise along with the temperature. In the summertime, Salvador sizzles with lively ambiance, myriad musical shows, open rehearsals of Carnaval *blocos,* and especially the "season" of popular *festas.* If revelry, combined with relaxation, is what you're looking for, you've come to the right place. With the end of Carnaval comes what Soteropolitanos refer to as the post-Carnaval *ressaca* (hangover), which means a halt in the partying until June and a return to work. Mother Nature also seems to know that the party is over, because the period from April to June is usually rainy. Bahian "winter," which stretches from June-September, is a great time to visit the city and the coastal regions as well as the Chapada. Although short, sudden downpours are common, the sun shines less intensely. Except for mid-July-August, which coincides with Brazilian school vacation, hotels and beaches are less crowded— many Bahians think it odd to lie on a beach in the "middle of winter."

Salvador

Salvador was originally built around a cliff overlooking the Bay of All Saints, which effectively split the city into two. The Cidade Alta (Upper Town) was home to ornate administrative palaces and churches, while the Cidade Baixa (Lower Town) sheltered maritime docks and markets and later grew into the financial and commercial district. To this day, the two are linked by a series of tortuously steep roads, two funiculars, and one of Salvador's most famous monuments: the Elevador Lacerda.

Over time, the city grew, following the extension of the Cidade Alta's main commercial avenue, Avenida Sete de Setembro, which leads from the Praça do Sé in the colonial Pelourinho district to the main square of Campo Grande—an area that today is the Centro district. From Campo Grande, Avenida Sete de Setembro continues down to the lively beach neighborhood known as Barra; Barra's iconic black-and-white striped lighthouse marks the point at which the placid Bay of All Saints meets the rougher waters of the Atlantic open sea. At this point, the main coastal road takes over, continuing for 20 kilometers (12.5 mi) to the former fisherman's enclave of Itapuã, whose rustic charms were romanticized in the lyrics of two former residents, Dorival Caymmi and Vinicius de Moraes.

SIGHTS

Most of Salvador's sights are conveniently located in the old colonial center of the Cidade Alta, known as the Pelourinho (a reference to one of the neighborhood's main squares, the Largo do Pelourinho, where slaves were routinely whipped at the *pelourinho,* or "pillory").

★ Pelourinho

Despite its inauspicious past, the Pelourinho provides a feast for architecture buffs, with the largest concentration of baroque architecture in the Americas. Replete with richly adorned churches and convents, its hilly cobblestoned streets also reflect a lot of the vibrancy and color of Bahian life. Until the 1990s, the "Pelô" was a crumbling mess. After being declared a UNESCO World Heritage Site in 1985, the area underwent a massive restoration that saved many of the historic buildings and somewhat unceremoniously removed the former inhabitants, replacing them with boutiques, restaurants, bars, and open-air spaces for musical shows. What it lost in terms of gritty authenticity, it made up for in terms of heightened security and animation.

The Pelô has since become increasingly forsaken by locals, with the exception of vendors and beggars who approach anybody resembling a tourist. Nonetheless, there is no denying the rich history and magnificence of its restored edifices. While the *bairro* can be explored on foot in a couple of hours, in order to take advantage of all the church interiors and museums, boutiques, and lazy outdoor bars, you'll need a full day. The labyrinthine layout of the neighborhood is conducive to wandering. Just make sure you don't venture off the beaten police-patrolled track, especially at night; tourist *assaltos* (muggings) are not unheard of.

PRAÇA MUNICIPAL

The seat of colonial Brazil for over two centuries, the Pelourinho is dominated by the monumental Palácio do Rio Branco (tel. 71/3316-6928, 10:30am-1:30pm and 2:30am-5:30pm Mon.-Fri., 1pm-6pm Sat.-Sun., free). Guarded by soaring eagles and topped by an impressive dome, the palace is fondly known by Bahians as the *bolo de noiva* ("the wedding cake"), an appropriate nickname considering its resemblance to the baker's confection. Constructed by Tomé de Souza in 1549 as the governor's palace, over time the building suffered partial demolitions and makeovers, which explains its eclectic style—a mixture of neoclassical, Byzantine, and Renaissance elements. Having housed the Portuguese royal family when they fled Napoleon's troops in 1808, and later a prison, it now houses Bahia's ministry of culture. Step inside for a guided tour and you'll find rococo plasterwork, frescoes, and a small museum. More interesting is the view from

the palace's verandas, which takes in the Cidade Baixa and the Bay of All Saints.

ELEVADOR LACERDA

The streamlined, art deco Elevador Lacerda (6:30am-11pm daily, R$0.15), to the right of the Palácio do Rio Branco, has shuttled lines of Soteropolitanos between the Cidade Baixa and the Cidade Alta since the 1930s. It takes only 20 seconds for each of its four elevators to transport more than 50,000 passengers a day. To visit the Mercado Modelo, catch a local bus to Bonfim, or grab a boat to Itaparica, the Elevador comes in handy. Otherwise, have a seat at Sorveteria Cubana (tel. 71/3322-7000, 9am-10pm), a 1930s landmark, and indulge in an icy treat such as a *coco espumante* (a fizzy old-fashioned coconut ice cream soda).

MUSEU DA MISERICÓRDIA

Down the Rua da Misericórdia, past City Hall, is the Museu da Misericórdia (Rua da Misericórida 6, tel. 71/3322-7355, 10am-5pm Mon.-Fri., 9am-1pm Sun., R$6). A religious complex dating from 1549, it was converted into a museum as part of an ongoing project to renovate the architectural treasures on this strip. A permanent exhibition of artwork, religious objects, and furniture from the 17th-19th centuries conjures up Salvador's colonial history, as do its magnificent cloisters, church, and living quarters.

GALERIA FUNDAÇÃO PIERRE VERGER

The Galeria Fundação Pierre Verger (Portal da Misericórdia 9, tel. 71/3321-2341, www.pierreverger.org, 9am-8pm Mon.-Sat., 9am-3pm Sun., free), across from the Museu da Misericórdia, shows a small rotating collection of black-and-white photographs by French photographer, ethnographer, and adopted Bahian Pierre Verger. Born into a wealthy Parisian milieu in which he never felt at home, in 1932 Verger took off at the age of 30 to explore the world. With a camera in hand to fund his journeys (his pictures were published in magazines such as *Life* and

Pelourinho and Centro

R VISCONDE DE MAIA
R DO SODRE
LAD DA PREGUIÇA
AV CONTORNO
LAD CONCEIÇÃO

AMADO
To Museu de Arte Moderna (MAM), Castro Alves, Museu de Arte da Bahia, and Museu Carlos Costa Pinto

MUSEU DE ARTE SACRA DA BAHIA

BECO C MARIA DA PAZ

Praça Castro Alves

IGREJA N S DA CONCEIÇÃO DA PRAIA

MERCADO MODELO
Praça Cairu
R BELGICA

To Campo Grande and Barra

MOSTEIRO DE SÃO BENTO

R BARBOSA

MINI CACIQUE

PALÁCIO RIO BRANCO

ELEVADOR LACERDA

SANTOS DUMONT
CORPO SANTO

HORTAS
R DO TESOURO
RUA CHILE

Praça Tomé de Sousa

MUSEU DA MISERICORDIA

MONTANHA
R DA PE NOBREGA

R DO PARAISO
R DA CASTANHEDA

CENTRO
AJUDA
SALDANHA
CURRIACHITO

LAD DA PRAÇA
DA GAMA
GUEDES

GALERIA FUNDAÇÃO PIERRE VERGER

O CRAVINHO

CATEDRAL BASÍLICA
Praça da Sé

IGREJA DE SÃO PAULO DOS CLERIGOS

MUSEU AFRO-BRASILEIRO
ALFREDO BRITO
CASA DO AMARELINDO
AXEGO

MOURARIA

PALMA

KOISA NOSSA

R 28 DE SETEMBRO
R S FRANCISCO
BRITO
OPRAÇÃO DE MAIO

R DO BISPO
CRUZEIRO S FRANCISCO

Terreiro de Jesus

JOÃO DE DEUS
C REBELO

MANGUEIRA
BENGALA
R DA INDEPENDENCIA

CIDADE ALTA
SEABRA
SANTANA
BARRO DO DESTERRO

IGREJA E CONVENTO DE SÃO FRANCISCO

GLACIER LAPORTE

DOMINGOS DE GUSMÃO

IGREJA DA ORDEM TERCEIRA DE SÃO

IGREJA DA ORDEM TERCEIRA DE SÃO FRANCISCO

HOTEL VILLA BAHIA
ALAIDE DO FEIJÃO
LA FIGA
PONTO VITAL

GREGORIO
LADAN FILHAS
LAPANH DE MATOS

HOSTEL GALERIA 13

MUSEU DA CERAMICA UDO KNOFF
MUSEU TEMPOSTAL
MUSEU ABELARDO RODRIGUES

R TINGUI
R DO CARRO
STA CLARA
R DO DESTERRO
PRATA
PTE DO DESTERRO
R DA POEIRA
JENIPAPEIRO
LAD DA SAUDE
JOGO DO LOURENÇO

JOANA ANGELICA

0 200 yds
0 200 m

© AVALON TRAVEL

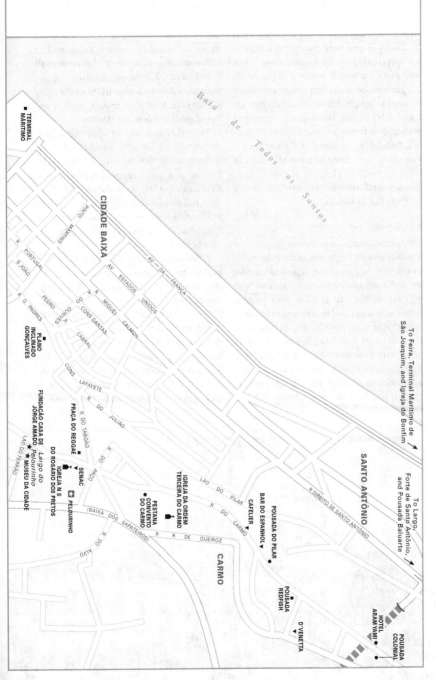

Baía de Todos os Santos

■ TERMINAL MARITIMO

CIDADE BAIXA

R PINTO
MARTINS
R PORTUGAL
S. JOÃO
R G PADRES GONÇALVES
PEDRO
■ PLANO INCLINADO GONÇALVES
DUNES A
DO
CABRAL
CONS DANTAS
R MIGUEL CALMON
AV ESTADOS UNIDOS
AV — DA — FRANÇA

CONS LAFAYETE
R DO JULIÃO
PRAÇA DO REGGAE ■
R DO TABOÃO
FUNDAÇÃO CASA DE JORGE AMADO
IGREJA N S DO ROSÁRIO DOS PRETOS
SENAC ✚
■ SENAC
● PELOURINHO
Largo do Pelourinho ★
★ MUSEU DA CIDADE
LAD DO FERRÃO
R DO PAÇO
R DO ALVO
(BAIXA DOS SAPATEIROS)

PESTANA CONVENTO DO CARMO ●
IGREJA DA ORDEM TERCEIRA DO CARMO
R DE QUEIROZ
R DO CARMO
LAD DO PILAR
CARMO

To Largo, Terminal Marítimo de São Joaquim, and Igreja do Bonfim ↗

SANTO ANTÔNIO

R DIREITO SÉ SANTO ANTÔNIO

BAR DO ESPANHOL ▼
CAFELIER ▼
POUSADA DO PILAR ▼

To Largo, Forte de Santo Antônio, and Pousada Baluarte ↗

POUSADA REDFISH ●

D'VENETTA ▼

HOTEL ARAMYAMI ●

POUSADA COLONIAL ●

Paris Match), he traveled throughout Asia, Africa, and the Americas. In Bahia, he felt a strong bond that kept luring him back until he finally settled here, becoming a professor specializing in the African diaspora as well as a Candomblé initiate. In the 1940s Verger was one of the first people permitted to make photographic records of mysterious Candomblé rituals. His elegantly composed yet highly sensual portraits of Salvador's sailors, fishermen, *capoeiristas,* Carnaval merrymakers, and Bahians from all walks of life offer precious glimpses of a world past. The small gift store has eye-catching Verger T-shirts and handbags.

TERREIRO DE JESUS

The impressive square known as Terreiro de Jesus marks the beginning of the Pelourinho district. Try to ignore the exaggeratedly made-up, turbaned, and petticoated Bahianas who will encourage you to have your picture taken with them and focus on the cluster of remarkable religious edifices, starting with the Catedral Basílica (Sé) (tel. 71/3321-4573, 9am-5pm Mon.-Sat., 1pm-5pm Sun., R$3). An eclectic mélange of baroque, rococo, and neoclassical styles, the 17th-century cathedral was built out of sandstone shipped in blocks from Portugal before undergoing reconstruction after an early 20th-century fire. Its splendid interior is a testament to the riches of Portugal's overseas colonies. The 16th-century ceramic tiles in the sacristy hail from Macau, while the delicate ivory and tortoiseshell inlay in one altar (third on the right) is from Goa. Marble, jacaranda, and lots and lots of gold leaf adorn the interior.

Two other churches sit upon the square: the Igreja da Ordem Terceira de São Domingos de Gusmão (tel. 71/3242-4185, 8:30am-noon and 1:30pm-6pm Mon.-Thurs, R$2) dates to 1731, while the cocktail of rococo and neoclassical that is the Igreja São Pedro dos Clérigos (8am-noon and 2pm-7pm Mon.-Sat., free) was conceived in the 19th century.

Adjacent to the cathedral is a grand building that housed Brazil's first school of medicine, founded in 1833. Today, it shelters the compelling Museu Afro-Brasileiro (tel. 71/3283-5540, 9am-5pm Mon.-Fri., R$6). Along with maps tracing the trade routes that brought African slaves to Bahia, exhibits of objects and artifacts draw parallels between African and Bahian cultural traditions, including capoeira and Candomblé. A highlight is the collection of sacred objects

Terreiro de Jesus

and apparel—as well as photos—related to Candomblé and the cult of individual *orixás,* or divinities, which provide an informative introduction to the Afro-Brazilian religion that is such a strong cultural reference in Bahia. Depicting the *orixás* are the exquisitely carved wooden panels, inlaid with shells and shiny metals, sculpted by one of Bahia's most famous artists, Carybé.

★ IGREJA E CONVENTO DE SÃO FRANCISCO

Looming magnificently at the far end of Largo do Cruzeiro de São Francisco is the finest example of Bahian baroque architecture: a religious complex dedicated to Saint Francis of Assisi comprising two churches and a convent. Constructed between 1686 and 1750, the Igreja e Convento de São Francisco (tel. 71/3322-6430, 9am-5:30pm Mon. and Wed.-Sat., 9am-4pm Tues., 10am-3pm Sun., R$5) will take your breath away with gold leaf paneling—800 kilograms (1,760 pounds), to be exact—that covers its intricately carved and sumptuously painted ceilings and altars. Carefully wrought scenes depict the life of Saint Francis on 55,000 blue-and-white Portuguese azulejos in the chapel and cloister. Tuesday mass is followed by the distribution of food to the poor, which then morphs into a Pelô-wide celebration of a more profane nature, known as *terça do Benção* (Tuesday of the Blessing).

★ IGREJA DA ORDEM TERCEIRA DE SÃO FRANCISCO

Next door to the Igreja e Convento de São Francisco, the Igreja da Ordem Terceira de São Francisco (tel. 71/3321-6968, 8am-5pm daily, R$5), completed in 1703, is remarkable for its striking high-relief facade: a sandstone tapestry of saints, angels, and organic and abstract motifs. This unique exterior was "hidden" for 150 years until, in 1936, a painter accidentally discovered it when he chipped off a piece of the plaster facade. Inside the church, azulejo panels narrate the marriage of the king of Portugal's son to an Austrian princess and offer a rare portrait of Lisbon before it was devastated by the Great Earthquake of 1755.

MUSEU DA CERÁMICA UDO KNOFF

The Museu da Cerámica Udo Knoff (Rua Frei Vicente 3, tel. 71/3117-6389, noon-6pm Tues.-Fri., noon-5pm Sat.-Sun., free) displays a resplendent collection of ceramic tiles from Portugal, Spain, Belgium, and Mexico as well as Brazil. They are from the personal collection of Horst Udo Knoff, a German expat ceramicist whose own works, inspired by azulejos covering facades of Salvador's buildings, are also featured. To get here from the Igreja, follow Rua Inácio Acciole and take a left on Rua Frei Vicente.

MUSEU TEMPOSTAL

The "artwork" in the Museu Tempostal (Rua Gregório de Matos 33, tel. 71/3117-6383, noon-6pm Tues.-Fri., noon-5pm Sat.-Sun., free) consists of thousands of postcards that trace Salvador's surprisingly rapid transformation over the last century. The entire collection of more than 35,000 works includes some amazing belle epoque specimens—postcards decorated with embroidery as well as watercolors, feathers, and strands of human hair.

MUSEU ABELARDO RODRIGUES

The gracious 17th-century mansion known as the Solar do Ferrão houses the Museu Abelardo Rodrigues (Rua Gregório de Matos 45, tel. 71/3117-6467, 10am-6pm Tues.-Sun., R$1), a collection of more than 800 icons of saints, altars, engravings, and other religious objects (not all on display). The works were amassed by Pernambucano collector Abelardo Rodrigues, who resided here, and are considered to be one of the finest collections of sacred art in Brazil. Also on permanent display are architect Lina Bo Bardi's fine collection of Northeast Brazilian folk art and an equally impressive ensemble of African masks and statues donated by Italian magnate Claudio Masella.

LARGO DO PELOURINHO

When you first set foot in this picturesque square, you'll likely be overwhelmed by the baroque landscape of church spires and faded pastel mansions, as well as the Cubist-like image of houses rising up and down the Pelô's steep hills. Although its official name is Praça José de Alencar, it is known as Largo do Pelourinho due to its dubious past as the site of the city's *pelourinho* (whipping post; public flogging was legal in Brazil until 1835).

Today the *largo* buzzes with less nefarious activities. By day, vendors hawk *naïf* canvases and coax gringos to put Afro braids and corn-rows in their hair. Nights are filled with the pounding drums of traditional Afro-Bahian *blocos* such as Olodum, whose rhythms defy people to dance.

Housed in a handsome colonial mansion, the Museu da Cidade (Largo do Pelourinho 3, tel. 71/3321-1967, 9am-6pm Mon. and Wed.-Fri., R$1) serves up an eclectic mix of things Soteropolitano. Depictions of Catholic saints and ex-votos mingle with sculptures of *orixás* and other objects related to Candomblé. More secular offerings include works by local artists and artisans and a room devoted to Castro Alves, one of Brazil's great romantic poets and famously eloquent abolitionists.

Next door, the Fundação Casa de Jorge Amado (Largo do Pelourinho 49, tel. 71/3321-0122, www.fundacaojorgeamado.com.br, 10am-6pm Mon.-Sat., free) is a small museum and shrine devoted to the life, times, and writing of Jorge Amado, one of Bahia's (and Brazil's) most cherished and internationally renowned writers. With photos, book covers, and other media featuring the author of *Dona Flor and Her Two Husbands* and *Gabriela, Clove and Cinnamon,* the museum provides an overview of Amado's life and career, also touching on that of his lifelong love and companion, Zélia Gattai, a renowned writer in her own right to whom homage is paid at the homonymous, and pleasant, café.

Halfway down the Largo, the strikingly blue-tinged Igreja Nossa Senhora do Rosário dos Pretos (tel. 71/3326-9701, 8:30am-6pm Mon.-Fri., 8:30am-3pm Sat.-Sun.) is a symbol of black pride and resistance. After the king of Portugal gave the site to the Irmandade dos Homens Pretos, a brotherhood of local black men, it took slaves most of the 18th century to construct this church. While the façade is classic rococo, the unusual tiled towers bear Indian influences, a consequence of Portugal's colony in Goa. Services in which Catholics hymns merge with traditional African percussion instruments (mass 6pm Tues.) reflect Bahia's unique religious syncretism.

IGREJA DA ORDEM TERCEIRA DO CARMO E CONVENTO DO CARMO

The climb up the Ladeira do Carmo might leave you huffing and puffing, but great views of the surrounding Pelô compensate. Halfway up, the majestic Escadas do Carmo staircase leads to the sadly dilapidated Igreja Santíssimo Sacramento do Passo. Both the staircase and the church were immortalized in the first Brazilian film to win the Cannes Festival's Palme d'Or, *O Pagador de Promessas* (1962).

Towering above the Ladeira do Carmo is the dramatic whitewashed complex that houses the Igreja da Ordem Terceira do Carmo (tel. 71/3481-4169, 8am-noon and 2pm-6pm Mon.-Sat., 8am-10am Sun., R$1) and the Convento do Carmo. Constructed in 1636 and rebuilt in neoclassical style after a fire in 1786, the church is worth a visit for its eerily expressive cedar carving of Christ, sculpted in 1730 by Francisco Xavier Chagas. A slave nicknamed "O Cabra" ("The Goat"), Chagas has been compared to the great *mulato* baroque sculptor of Minas Gerais, Aleijadinho. If the drops of blood on the reclining Christ figure seem to glint and glisten as if they were transparent liquid, it is because they are assembled out of 2,000 encrusted rubies. Chagas is also responsible for the statue of Nossa Senhora do Carmo, whose features were said to be inspired by Isabel, daughter of

Garcia d'Ávila, the largest landowner in the Northeast during colonial times.

Adjacent to the church is the Convento do Carmo (Rua do Carmo 1, www.pestana.com/en/pestana-convento-do-carmo). Built in 1586, this convent has been converted into a hotel. Wander in and examine the stylishly furnished interior, then stop for a drink at the bar-lounge that sprawls around a palmy, arcaded cloister.

Santo Antônio

Santo Antônio Além do Carmo is the name given to the narrow neighborhood that stretches from the church and convent of Carmo down to the open square of Largo do Santo Antônio. Neither as old, splendid, nor reupholstered as the Pelourinho, tranquil Santo Antônio hints at what the Pelô could have been had the strategies accompanying its makeover—expulsion of residents and pandering to tourists—not been so brutal. In the last few years, many of its crumbling belle epoque-era mansions have been saved by enterprising hoteliers who have opened up restaurants, galleries, and *pousadas*. Instead of radically transforming the 'hood, these newcomers spruced it up and then integrated themselves into the fabric of what is still, at heart, a traditional *bairro popular*. As you make your way down the main street, Rua Direito de Santo Antônio, highlights include the Cruz do Pascoal, a giant cross planted in the middle of the road, and the beguiling 18th-century Igreja Nossa Senhora do Boqueirão (Rua Direito de Santo Antônio 60).

Largo de Santo Antônio is framed at one end by a belvedere overlooking the ocean and at the other by the neoclassical Igreja de Santo Antônio Além do Carmo. The church is almost always open due to Santo Antônio's popularity—not only a protector of the poor, he also intercedes on behalf of lonely hearts and bachelors (as the patron saint of marriage) and specializes in finding lost valuables.

At the far side of the square, the Forte de Santo Antônio Além do Carmo (Largo de Santo Antônio, tel. 71/3321-7587, 7:30pm-9:30pm Tues., Thurs., and Sat., 5:30pm-7:30pm Sun., free) was constructed in the 16th century by the Portuguese as a defensive measure against invading Dutch troops. During the years of military dictatorship, the abandoned fort served as a detention center for political prisoners who spoke out against the government. Today it shelters the Capoeira Preservation Center, dedicated to safeguarding this traditional martial art while providing new headquarters for some of the city's oldest capoeira schools.

Cidade Baixa

Sadly, the Cidade Baixa, Salvador's port and commercial district, has seen better days. The area is a mélange of decaying historic buildings and decaying high-rises built before Salvador's commercial center moved to the neighborhoods surrounding Shopping Iguatemi. Today, "Comércio" (as it is known) is fairly bustling during the day but dangerous at night. Take a bus, the Elevador Lacerda to Praça Visconde de Cairu, or a taxi. Don't even think about walking up or down the steep roads linking the two *cidades*—they are unsafe, even by day.

IGREJA DE NOSSA SENHORA DA CONCEIÇÃO DA PRAIA

The stately, baroque Igreja de Nossa Senhora da Conceição da Praia (Rua Conceição da Praia, tel. 71/3242-0545, 7am-noon and 3pm-7pm Mon., 7am-5pm Tues.-Fri., 7am-11:30am Sat.-Sun., free) rises to the left upon emerging from the Elevador Lacerda. Built in Portugal in 1736, the deconstructed church was shipped piece by piece to the site of Salvador's first chapel. The patron saint of Salvador, Our Lady of Conception, is also linked to the wildly popular Candomblé *orixá* Iemenjá, goddess of the sea. Accordingly, the saint's feast day (Dec. 8) is the occasion for one of the city's most traditional religious and popular *festas*.

IGREJA DE NOSSO
SENHOR DO BONFIM

If you hop a bus with the destination Bonfim or Ribeira from Praça Cairu, or Campo Grande, you will find yourself sailing through the length of the Cidade Baixa, following the 8-kilometer (5-mi) route taken by worshippers and revelers who, on the second Thursday of January, make their way in a procession to one of Brazil's most famous churches: the Igreja de Nosso Senhor do Bonfim (Praça Senhor do Bonfim, tel. 71/3316-2196, 6:30am-noon and 2pm-6pm Tues.-Sun.).

Sacred to Catholics as well as followers of Candomblé (for whom Senhor do Bonfim is equated with both Christ and one of the most important *orixás,* Oxalá), the *igreja* is an important pilgrimage site. Morning mass is large, especially on Friday—Oxalá's day of the week. Rising up from a hilltop and accessorized by swaying imperial palms, it's an eye-catching example of Portuguese rococo. In front, you'll likely be accosted by a few vendors plying you with brightly colored *fitas de Bonfim.* If you choose to follow tradition and tie one of these ribbons around your wrist, make sure you tie three knots and make a wish on each one. You'll be stuck wearing it for weeks, months, or even years (don't tie it too tight); when it naturally falls off, your wishes will come true. With the exception of the resplendent panels of blue-and-white Portuguese tiles, the interior of the church is relatively unadorned by Bahian standards. The real interest lies in its importance to Bahians, which becomes clear when you visit the church's small but fascinating Museu dos Ex-Votos do Senhor do Bonfim (Largo do Bonfim, tel. 71/3312-4512, 9am-noon and 2pm-5pm Tues.-Sat., R$2).

Your visit begins in the Sala dos Milagres (Room of Miracles), whose walls are covered from floor to ceiling with thousands of photographs and handwritten notes accompanied by *fitas de Bonfim.* These heartfelt supplications to Senhor do Bonfim—be it pleading for the life of a child, the safe return of a fisherman, or even victory in a soccer championship—are incredibly moving. So are the photos, newspaper clippings, and paintings of miracles, depicting believers being saved from tragedies such as car accidents and fires. Dangling from the ceiling are wooden and plastic heads, limbs, and even organs. These are the offerings of worried patients seeking protection before surgery. The second floor houses older and more precious ex-votos in display cases—including silver heads, arms, hearts, eyes, noses, even livers and intestines—offered in thanks by miraculously cured patients. The presence of soccer uniforms indicates that both of Salvador's major teams wouldn't dream of starting *futebol* season without first visiting the church for a blessing.

FORTE DE MONTE SERRAT
AND PONTA DE HUMAITÁ

If you walk uphill from the Largo de Bonfim and take the road that swerves to the left, you'll be treated to sweeping panoramic views of the entire city. Follow the road for another five minutes, which will lead you downhill to the popular beach of Boa Viagem. A favorite *praia popular,* on weekends it is so packed with residents of surrounding neighborhoods you can barely see the sand. Crowning the beach is the 16th-century Forte de Monte Serrat, whose cannons chased off invading Dutch. Today, its functions are decidedly less bellicose—it is a favorite place for smooching couples to get a glimpse of the sunset over the Bay of All Saints. Another great vantage point is the nearby Ponta de Humaitá, whose striped lighthouse, tiny 17th-century Igreja de Nossa Senhora de Monte Serrat, and sweeping sea views provide a romantic spot for a late-afternoon drink.

Centro

Salvador's Centro encompasses a somewhat loosely defined neighborhood that more or less consists of the old "downtown" of the Cidade Alta, which follows Avenida Sete de Setembro (the main drag) from its beginning at Praça Castro Alves to Campo Grande and the sweeping tree-lined Corredor da Vitória. Chaotic, crowded, and oddly provincial for such a major city, Centro remains an interesting place to walk around. Filled with museums, churches, shops, markets, and *ambulantes* (street vendors), by day it hums with activity but at night empties out and is dangerous to stroll around in.

From the Praça Municipal, the once elegant Rua Chile still displays some grandiose buildings that formerly housed department stores and hotels. Restoration projects are underway in an attempt to regain at least some of its former glory. Rua Chile leads onto the Praça Castro Alves, a semicircular plaza where Bahia's famous Romantic poet (Antônio Frederico de Castro Alves) stares out at the Bay of All Saints.

MUSEU DE ARTE SACRA DA BAHIA

A block from Praça Castro Alves, Ladeira de Santa Teresa is a steep little alley that plunges down to the imposing 17th-century convent of Santa Teresa de Ávila, which was once occupied by the Ordem das Carmelitas Descalços (Barefoot Carmelites Order). Overlooking the sea and surrounded by shady courtyards, its tranquil church, cloisters, and monks' cells are part of the Museu de Arte Sacra da

Bahia (Rua do Sodré 276, tel. 71/3243-6511, 11:30am-5pm Mon.-Fri., R$5). One of the most important and impressive museums of sacred religious art in Brazil, its collection of 1,400 pieces includes a wealth of paintings, sculptures, icons, and furniture from Bahia's glorious colonial past.

MOSTEIRO DE SÃO BENTO

Along Avenida Sete de Setembro, a few meters from Praça Castro Alves, is one of the oldest monasteries in the Americas. The grandiose Mosteiro de São Bento (Largo de São Bento, tel. 71/2106-5200, 11:30am-5pm daily) has undergone numerous renovations since its founding in 1582. Pop in for a quick look at its interior and museum of religious art or take a cab here on Sunday to hear the monastery's 30 cloistered monks sing Gregorian chants.

MUSEU DE ARTE MODERNA

Take a quick taxi ride up the coastal road to one of the city's finest and most beautifully situated museums, the Museu de Arte Moderna (MAM; Av. Contorno, tel. 71/3117-6139, www.bahiamam.org, 1pm-7pm Tues.-Fri. and Sun., 1pm-10pm Sat., free). Originally titled the Solar do Unhão, this 17th-century complex hovering over the Bay of All Saints

Barra lighthouse

was a sugarcane plantation complete with a mansion (*solar*), slave quarters, and a chapel. In the 1960s, the well-preserved ensemble got an inspired refurbishment courtesy of São Paulo modernist architect Lina Bo Bardi that transformed it into Bahia's Museum of Modern Art. A permanent collection boasts token works of major Brazilian modernist painters, and the museum showcases temporary exhibitions of contemporary artists from all over Brazil.

The buildings and setting are captivating. A sculpture garden, featuring works by local talents such as Carybé and Mario Cravo Jr., winds along a shady path overlooking the sea. In the late afternoon, the wooden pier above the ocean is a magical place to watch the sun set behind the Ilha da Itaparica. Shaded by flamboyant trees, it is the scene of Saturday night jazz jams (from 6pm, R\$6) that are mobbed by young Soteropolitanos.

CAMPO GRANDE

This elegant oasis of a park boasts carefully tended flower patches, century-old trees, playgrounds, goldfish ponds, and plenty of benches from where you can take it all in. At the center of Campo Grande, the Monumento ao Dois de Julho, featuring a statue of a fierce-looking Caboclo (a mythical figure, part Indian, part African, who is a symbol of Bahian independence from the Portuguese), pays homage to July 2, 1823, the date Bahian troops achieved autonomy by expelling Portuguese troops. The monument—and Campo Grande—has a strong symbolic significance for Soteropolitanos. Accordingly, a large number of important official and cultural events are often held here.

Corredor da Vitória

From Campo Grande onward, Avenida Sete de Setembro is known as the Corredor da Vitória. Lined with wonderfully overgrown trees and less wonderful luxury apartment complexes, "Vitória" is where Salvador's elite have traditionally lived. The small but economically important British community

that founded this posh hood in the late 19th century and constructed some of its lavish mansions (a few still survive) is now home to a handful of small museums and cultural centers.

MUSEU DE ARTE DA BAHIA

Occupying a stately 1920s mansion, the Museu de Arte da Bahia (Av. Sete de Setembro 2340, tel. 71/3117-6903, 2pm-7pm Tues.-Fri., 2:30pm-6:30pm Sat.-Sun., R\$5, free Thurs. and Sun.) houses a hit-and-miss collection of Bahian paintings and furnishings as well as some curiosities, such as a sewing machine that transforms into a small piano.

MUSEU CARLOS COSTA PINTO

In a gracious private villa that still belongs to Salvador's traditional Costa Pinto family, the Museu Carlos Costa Pinto (Av. Sete de Setembro 2490, tel. 71/3336-6081, 2:30pm-7pm Wed.-Mon., R\$5, free Thurs.) features a rare and magnificent collection of Bahian art and artifacts that offer a glimpse into the grandeur of the Bahian elite during colonial times. Apart from some exquisite European furnishings and finery, you're likely to be most impressed by the fantastic collection of *balangandãs:* ornate bracelets with glittery, dangling "charms" ranging from tropical fruits to *figas* (clenched fists symbolizing power). Made of silver and gold, these were gifts given by rich masters to their female slaves, who used them to accessorize their traditional attire of white petticoats and turbans. After feasting your eyes, retire to the lovely courtyard Balangandan Café and savor some of the menu's delicious French tarts.

PALACETE DAS ARTES

In the early 20th century, businessman Bernardo Catharino was the richest man in Bahia. In 1912, he built this gracious mansion in the still swanky neighborhood of Graça (just off the Corredor da Vitória). Known today as the Palacete das Artes (Rua da Graça 284, Graça, tel. 71/3117-6910, www.

palacetedasartes.ba.gov.br, 10am-6pm Wed.-Mon., free), it's worth checking out for the intricate parquet floors, jewel-hued stained glass windows, belle epoque frescoes, and the exhibits of modern and contemporary Brazilian art displayed in the villa as well as an adjacent modern annex. Shaded by giant mango trees, the gardens can be savored from the outdoor Solar Café.

Barra

At the end of Corredor de Vitória, the descent from Avenida Sete de Setembro begins a steep plunge toward the neighborhood and beaches of Barra. On the way down, you'll pass Bahia's yacht club, with its swan-like array of sailboats, the Cimetério dos Ingleses, where Bahia's Brit expat community encountered a scenic resting place, and, perched on a verdant hill, the 16th-century Igreja de Santo Antônio da Barra.

PORTO DA BARRA

Salvador's small but famous urban beach, Porto da Barra, is dramatically framed by two 17th-century Portuguese fortresses: Forte São Diogo and Forte Santa Maria. More than just a small crescent-shaped golden sand beach, "Porto" is an entire microcosm uniting families, gays, tourists, locals, vendors, hustlers, lovers, celebrities, sun worshippers, and volleyball and frescoball aficionados on one vibrant and colorful strip of sand bathed by the calm and surprisingly clear sea. Barring the rainy season, no matter how overpopulated it gets, Porto's waters are always miraculously crystalline.

Although Porto has a small-town feel to it—aided by the fact that the only vessels bobbing on its waters are brightly painted wooden fishing boats—it packs a surprisingly urban wallop. You'll be bombarded by the songs and chants of passing vendors hawking everything from handmade jewelry to fresh fruit popsicles called *picolés* (the best are made by a company called Capelinha). You'll also be spoiled: After renting a beach chair and giant parasol, you'll have your feet regularly refreshed with a watering can and all your drink requests attended to.

Porto is the classic place to watch the sunset—applause rings out the moment the glowing orange-red disk descends below the Ilha da Itaparica, bathing both sky and sea in a painterly blaze of colors. (On Friday nights in summer, sunset is accompanied by free outdoor concerts). Since the beach is lit at night, it is possible to take a moonlight dip. However, be very careful with your valuables (even more so than during the day), since tourists are often targeted by thieves.

FAROL DA BARRA

Walking along the breezy seaside promenade—past small coves and the increasing number of hotels, gyms, cybercafés, and bars that are turning Barra into a small-scale Copacabana—you'll soon reach the iconic black-and-white striped Barra lighthouse. Jutting out into the sea at the point where the Bay of All Saints meets the Atlantic, the Farol da Barra is lodged within the 17th-century Forte de Santo Antônio. Although the current lighthouse, constructed of iron, was built in 1836, the original wooden one—dating from 1696—operated using whale oil and was the first lighthouse in all of the Americas. Inside the fort, the Museu Naútico da Bahia (tel. 71/3264-3296, www.museunauticodabahia.org.br, 9am-7pm Tues.-Sun., R$6) displays maps, navigation instruments, model ships, and other seafaring paraphernalia. Just as interesting is the secluded bar situated within the lighthouse's sun-bleached walls. During the year, the Farol and surrounding area are the setting for various shows and concerts; the biggest occur on New Year's Eve and New Year's Day.

Rio Vermelho and Vicinity

Rio Vermelho is a bohemian enclave, more lively at night when its bars, squares, and restaurants fill with the city's artistic and intellectual crowd. Although its beaches aren't good for swimming, the hidden Praia do Buracão ("Big Hole") functions as a hip

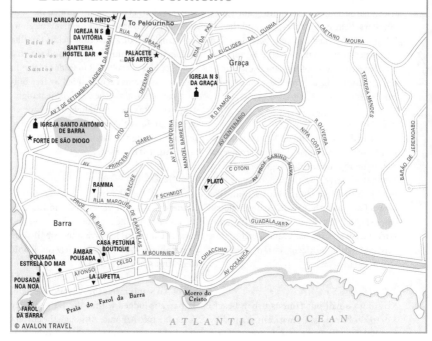

Barra and Rio Vermelho

To Pelourinho

MUSEU CARLOS COSTA PINTO ★
IGREJA N S DA VITÓRIA
SANTERIA HOSTEL BAR ●
PALACETE DAS ARTES ★

Baía de Todos os Santos

IGREJA N S DA GRAÇA

Graça

IGREJA SANTO ANTÔNIO DE BARRA
★ FORTE DE SÃO DIOGO

PLATÔ ▼

RAMMA ▼

Barra

CASA PETÚNIA BOUTIQUE
ÂMBAR POUSADA ●
POUSADA ESTRELA DO MAR ●
LA LUPETTA ▼
POUSADA NOA NOA

★ FAROL DA BARRA

Praia do Farol da Barra

Morro do Cristo

GUADALAJARA

A T L A N T I C   O C E A N

© AVALON TRAVEL

little beach hideout for old-time residents and young *alternativos*. The neighborhood is enhanced by cobblestoned squares where the city's triumvirate of reigning Bahianas sell their famed *acarajés* and *abarás*.

Rio Vermelho is followed by the rather soulless Pituba, where the city's yuppies live. From there, the beaches keep coming until Itapuã, which only a couple of decades ago was a bucolic palm-fringed fishing village that captivated the imaginations of residents such as Dorival Caymmi and Vinicius de Moraes, both of whom immortalized its languorous vibe in their unforgettable musical compositions. Today, the neighborhood is more developed and scruffy; it's not the best beach in town for a swim. Nonetheless, the languorous vibe has somehow survived—as have the fishermen, the swaying palms, and the pretty candy cane-striped lighthouse.

More popular with middle-class patrons (who have cars) are the more unspoiled beaches that follow: Stella Maris and Flamengo (municipal buses whose final destination is marked Praia de Flamengo depart from Campo Grande or along the *orla*). These beaches offer more shade, water-sports equipment, and natural pools that are ideal for kids.

Baía de Todos os Santos

It's the biggest bay in Brazil—even bigger than Rio's famous Guanabara Bay—and the beckoning blue and always warm waters of the Bay of All Saints are ideal for swimming, sailing, diving, and contemplation.

ILHA DE ITAPARICA

The largest of the bay's 30-plus islands is the 35-kilometer-long (22-mi) narrow strip called Itaparica, whose lithe silhouette bisects the sea and the sky for those gazing out over the bay from Salvador. A favorite getaway for Soteropolitanos, Itaparica's beaches are lined with many weekend and holiday homes—a

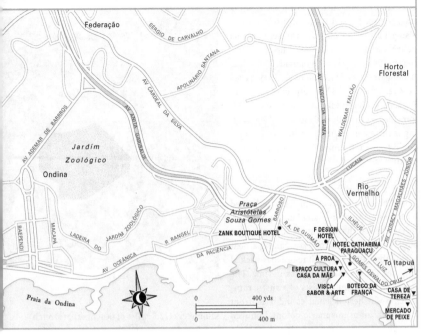

few quite old and grand, others resembling *favelas*. Avoid holiday weekends; getting there and back means lining up for hours to catch a boat (make sure you buy your return ticket), and once there, you'll be immersed in a sea of people. However, during the week or in off-season, the *"ilha"* has a laid-back atmosphere. Although the beaches are inferior to those north of Salvador, soaking in the calm blue water is as relaxing as taking a bath, and the view of the glimmering white city across the bay is quite enchanting. The island's major crop is mangoes, and once you sink your teeth into the real thing (depending on the season, they'll be literally raining down on you), you'll be in heaven.

There are two ways of getting from Salvador to Itaparica. The nicest, and simplest, is to grab a boat bound for Mar Grande at the Terminal Náutico da Bahia (Av. da França 757, tel. 71/3242-3180, R$4.20), behind the Mercado Modelo. The scenic trip across the bay takes 45 minutes with departures every 30 minutes 6:30am-8pm daily (depending on the tides). On the other side, Mar Grande is a lazy beach resort town with some languid old summer homes, tree-lined streets, and lots of seafood restaurants. You can easily explore the beaches by foot or rent a bike. The return trip at the end of the day almost always offers the bonus of a fantastic sunset.

Another way to get to Itaparica is to grab a catamaran or ferryboat from the Terminal Marítimo de São Joaquim (Av. Oscar Pontes 1501, tel. 71/3032-0475, www.agerba. ba.gov.br/transporteHidroviarioFerry.htm, R$3.95-5.20), near the Feira de São Joaquim. Although you can take a bus marked Ribeira or Bonfim, the easiest way to get to the ferry terminal is by taxi. Ferries will take you to Itaparica's main bus and boat terminal, aptly named Bom Despacho (Good Send-off). Ferry crossings take about an hour with departures every hour 5am-11:30pm daily.

From Bom Despacho, buses travel to cities on the Recôncavo as well as southern coast destinations such as Valença, Camamu, Itacaré, Ilhéus, and Porto Seguro. You can also get a *kombi* (collective van service) that delivers locals and beachgoers up and down the length of the island to individual beaches. Among the nicer destinations are Praia Ponta de Areia, north of Bom Despacho, as well as Praia da Penha and Barra Grande, several kilometers south of Bom Despacho. Also inviting is the colonial village of Itaparica, where you'll find a few remaining vestiges of 17th-century buildings.

ILHA DE MARÉ

Tiny Ilha de Maré is completely overlooked by tourists and even many Soteropolitanos. It hasn't been that long since the island got electricity, and in many ways taking a boat across the bay to its pristine beaches backed by green hills is like going back in time. The island's settlement consists of a rustic ramshackle of fisherfolk's houses and beachfront bars with an atmospheric colonial church thrown in for good measure. One of the main commercial products is the delicious *doce de banana,* a banana sweet made in wood ovens, then wrapped in banana-fiber packages and sold by the dozen by children roaming up and down the sand. On the beaches away from town, *barracas* serve delicious fried fish and *moqueca* as the tide comes in and laps at your legs.

To get a boat to Ilha de Maré, grab a bus with the destination Base Naval/São Tomé, which passes in front of the Teatro Castro Alves at Campo Grande; ride to the end of the line and then get a boat from the São Tomé de Paripe terminal (tel. 71/3307-1447). The R$3 trip takes 20 minutes with departures every 45 minutes 8am-5:30pm daily.

SPORTS AND RECREATION
Beaches

Barra marks the beginning of the *orla,* or coastline; a long string—roughly 20

Porto da Barra

kilometers (12.5 mi)—of beaches that stretch north to Itapuã and the city limits. Aside from Rio Vermelho, the adjoining neighborhoods themselves are of little interest. For good beaches, the ones farther away (beginning at Boca do Rio) are the only worthy candidates for bathing. Loads of buses leave from the center (Campo Grande and Lapa) or from Barra and speed up and down the coast all the way to Itapuã. On the weekends, particularly in the summer, all of these beaches get packed. It's best if you can go early and come back around 3pm to beat the crush.

Parks

Salvador is not a very green city. The only area resembling a park in the center of town is the Dique de Tororó, an urban lagoon out of whose calm waters rise gigantic statues of *orixás.* Surrounding the Dique is a walking and jogging path shaded by gigantic trees (and traffic). Kiosks sell *água de coco,* and it's possible to rent a pedal boat and glide around the water. The Dique's shores are flanked by

Avenida Presidente Silva e Costa and Avenida Vasco da Gama, and the lagoon is on the edge of the *bairros* of Nazaré and Tororó (behind the Lapa bus station).

Boat Excursions

Boats trips around the Bay of All Saints leave from Porto da Barra and from the ferry dock in front of the Mercado Modelo. The full-day excursions (around R$70 pp) stop at the larger islands, including Ilha dos Frades, Itaparica, and Ilha de Maré. Specific information is available at Salvador's largest hotels and at Bahiatursa, or contact a travel operator such as Privê Tur (tel. 71/3205-1400, www.privetur.com.br), which also runs various city tours.

Diving

If you want to search for buried treasure, there are about a dozen sunken ships in the Bay of All Saints. Dive Bahia (Porto da Barra 3809, tel. 71/3264-3820, www.divebahia.com.br) offers diving courses and rents out equipment, as does Bahia Scuba (Av. do Contorno 1010, Bahia Marina, tel. 71/3321-0156, www.bahiascuba.com.br). Dive excursion rates range R$150-210 pp (for certified divers) and R$250-280 (for beginners, which includes two dives).

Capoeira

This uniquely Brazilian activity is a graceful, but vigorous mix of dance and martial arts. Regular displays are held at the Mercado Modelo and the Terreiro de Jesus, but if it's an authentic experience you're after, head to one of the city's Academias de Capoeira.

One of the oldest capoeira schools, the Associação de Capoeira Mestre Bimba (Rua das Laranjeiras 1, Pelourinho, tel. 71/3322-0639, www.capoeiramestrebimba.com.br) offers demonstrations as well as classes open to visitors. The Forte de Santo Antônio Além do Carmo is occupied by the Centro Esportivo de Capoeira Angola (Largo de Santo Antônio, Santo Antônio, tel. 71/3117-1488), which houses seven different academies; apart from classes and demonstrations, capoeira-related events are always hosted here.

ENTERTAINMENT AND EVENTS
Nightlife

Salvador's nightlife is somewhat of an enigma. Contrary to its fame as a party place, when the sizzling summer season comes to an end, many bars and clubs close early or shut down altogether. Supposedly, the blame falls to the

Barra beach

fickleness of Soteropolitanos. There is always something happening in Barra and Rio Vermelho, and the Pelô and Centro offer a few old standbys that never go out of style. For listings, check out the entertainment sections of the two daily papers, *A Tarde* and *O Correio da Bahia,* or pick up the free monthly *Agenda Cultural* booklet available at tourist offices and cultural venues.

BARS

Most of Salvador's bars are at least partially outdoors and pretty basic. What makes them special is their strategic setting, located in a hidden garden or a colonial mansion, overlooking the ocean, or in a lively cobblestoned *praça.*

Although there's no lack of action in the Pelô, with vendors and beggars going after gringos some of it can be trying. Ubiquitous bars are sprinkled around the Praça Tereza Batista, Praça Pedro Archango, and Praça Quincas Berro D'Água. A traditional watering hole with a largely local clientele is O Cravinho (Terreiro de Jesus 3, Pelourinho, tel. 71/3322-6759, www.ocravinho.com.br, 11am-11pm daily). *Cravinho,* meaning "little clove," refers to the house specialty of *cachaça* infused with cloves, lime, and honey. This deceptively explosive concoction goes down nicely and costs next to nothing (which is why the bar is always packed). More than 200 such *cachaça* infusions (using herbs, flowers, roots, fruits, and seeds) are left to steep in the great wooden barrels lining the walls.

In Santo Antônio, a favorite place to watch the sunset over the Baía de Todos os Santos is the Bar do Espanhol, also known as Bar Cruz do Pascoal (Rua Direita de Santo Antônio 2, Santo Antônio, tel. 71/3243-2285, 11am-close Mon.-Sat.), where any hunger pangs can be assuaged by an *arrumadinho* (bite-size chunks of sun-dried beef mixed with black-eyed beans, toasted manioc flour, and diced tomatoes and peppers). A well-kept secret unknown to most locals, D'Venetta (Rua dos Adobes 12, tel. 71/3243-0616, www.dvenetta.com.br, 6pm-close Wed.-Sat.,

11am-6pm Sun.) is owned by a young local couple who had the insight to buy an enormous old house and transform it into the kind of bar where customers feel like family. Expect live samba and chorinho on the weekends and delicious home cooking all the time. The back garden with its wild roses and banana trees is an oasis.

Just behind the Pelourinho, Mouraria is a vibrant old neighborhood that is completely off the tourist path. For years, Thursday has been the customary night to head to one of the sidewalk bars clustered around Mouraria's cobblestoned square and dig into a ceramic pot steaming with *lambretas.* A local clam-like mollusk reputed to be an aphrodisiac (and a great hangover cure), the *lambretas* are steamed with cilantro and onions, then served piping hot. Traditionally, the city's "Old Guard" indulges at the square's largest bar, called Koisa Nossa (Travessa Engenheiro Alione 3, Mouraria, tel. 71/3266-5596, 5pm-close Mon.-Fri., noon-8pm Sat. More recently, a younger crowd has caught *lambreta* fever, and newer bars have opened to keep up with the demand.

Similar to Mouraria, Dois de Julho is another lively old residential neighborhood in the center of town where you can find authentic watering holes. One of the most happening is the Mocambinho Bar (Rua da Faisca 12, Dois de Julho, tel. 71/3328-1430, from 6pm Tues.-Sat.), a friendly place that draws in a bohemian and alternative crowd and where the home-cooked bar food—sun-dried beef and pumpkin puree, for example—is a few steps above usual bar fare.

In Barra, the biggest concentration of nocturnal activity takes place near the residential streets of Rua Belo Horizonte, Rua Florianópolis, and Rua Recife—a neighborhood known as Jardim Brasil. Although quiet enough during the week, the place sizzles on weekends. This is when a rather yuppie-ish university-age crowd flocks to the multiple bars and eateries in the area (which close early, at 1:30am). For a quieter and less collegiate option, drop by Platô (Rua Plínio

Moscoso 25, Barra, tel. 71/3273-1604, 5pm-close Tues.-Fri., noon-2am Sat., noon-10pm Sun.), an appealingly laid-back *boteco* with scrumptious food and killer drinks such as *pinha* (sugar apple) *caipis*. The tables sprinkled beneath the 50-year-old mango tree are a fine perch from which to zone out to live MPB and jazz on weekend afternoons.

The most eclectic nightlife destination in town is the bohemian *bairro* of Rio Vermelho. Unless it's pouring, the outdoor bars on Largo de Santana and Largo de Mariquita have always long lines of people waiting. The bars and restaurants on Rua da Paciência and Rua do Meio are always pulsing with activity. Considered one of the best traditional *botecos* in the *bairro,* the always popular but not too trendy Boteco da França (Rua Borges dos Reis 24-A, Rio Vermelho, tel. 71/3334-2734, 6pm-1am Mon., noon-close Tues.-Sun.) was opened in 2002 by a former waiter who toiled for many years at two other classic Rio Vermelho haunts. He obviously learned his trade well, because the Boteco offers attentive service, an extensive food and drink menu, including *chope de vinho* (wine on draft), and a mellow jazzy-bossa soundtrack that has made it a favorite with intellectuals, artists, and journalists. Cozy A Proa Bar (Rua Guedes Cabral 81, Rio Vermelho, tel. 71/8888-8315, 6pm-close Tues.-Sat.) is funkier, with a whitewashed porch that overlooks the sea and a narrow but homey interior that feels like a living room. If everything is closing down, the sun is coming up, and you're still raring to go, make a beeline for the Mercado de Peixe (Largo de Mariquita). Open 24 hours, this market's many lively bars are a classic "last call" option. Despite a soulless makeover, you'll still find plenty of traditional grub—try a thick, chowder-like bean soup, *caldo de feijão,* or *caldo de sururu* (similar to a mussel)—to stave off a hangover.

LIVE MUSIC

Salvador is justly famous for its music scene. There are limitless possibilities for hearing music, often for free. In the summertime,

especially, the Pelourinho throbs with the beat of drums as the city's Carnaval *blocos* (traditional Carnaval groups associated with organizations or neighborhoods) hold open weekly rehearsals, often with special guests in attendance. Usually beginning in November, these *ensaios* are either free or ridiculously expensive (to gouge tourists). Locales change yearly. Taking part will not only ensure you rub shoulders with Salvador's young blood but will also allow you to witness firsthand how summer musical hits—which eventually captivate all of Bahia and Brazil—are generated. Think of it as a taste of the sheer exuberance and intense musicality of Carnaval, should you not be around for the main event itself. The hottest *ensaios* around include the *tradiconalíssimo* Afro *blocos* Ilê Aiyê (whose rehearsals take place at its headquarters in the *bairro* of Curuzu), Filhos de Gandhy, Olodum, Muzenza, and Cortejo Afro (all of whom perform in the Pelô).

There is usually always something going on at the Pelourinho's Praça Tereza Batista and Praça Pedro Archango (both off Rua Gregório de Matos) as well as Praça Quincas Berro D'Água (off Rua Frei Vicente). In the summer, these three outdoor areas, surrounded by bars, host musical repertories ranging from samba-reggae to *pagode* that jive with the feverish public's desire to get down, get close, and samba till they drop. In the winter, the tempo slows down, switching to MPB, bossa nova, and *chorinho.* Not to be missed are the Tuesday-night jams on the steep steps of the Igreja do Santíssimo Sacramento do Passo on Rua do Passo, hosted by the terrific homegrown singer and composer Gerónimo. From the top of the stairs the view across the Pelourinho is enchanting, especially if there is a full moon. Also wildly popular are the traditional *rodas de samba* (samba circles), which take place in Largo de Santo Antônio at 7pm on the last Friday of the month.

Up and running since 1958, the beloved Concha Acústica (Ladeira da Fonte, Campo Grande, tel. 71/3535-0600, www.tca.ba.gov. br), or simply *a Concha,* is part of the Teatro

Castro Alves complex. Since day one, this outdoor amphitheater, which seats 5,000, has hosted the biggest names in Brazilian music and continues to do so, all at affordable prices.

On a much smaller scale, the Espaço Cultural Casa da Mãe (Rua Guedes Cabral 81, Rio Vermelho, tel. 71/3017-9041, 7pm-2am Tues.-Sat., 1pm-11pm Sun., cover R$5) is a cozy bar situated in a whitewashed house with ocean views. Operated by Roda Bahiana (an organization based in the Recôncavo town of Santo Amaro that promotes local artists and musicians), it is a great place to catch some very fine and authentic musical performances. For more space, stretch your legs or dance the night at neighboring Visca Sabor & Arte (Rua Guedes Cabral 123, Rio Vermelho, tel. 71/3034-1688, 6pm-2am Tues.-Sat.), a cool alternative with healthy bar grub.

NIGHTCLUBS

When Soteropolitanos want to let their hair down and samba the night away, they tend to favor the balmy outdoors over being cooped up between four walls. Because of this, the club scene can be rather uninspiring.

On a small street off Avenida Sete de Setembro (near Campo Grande), the Tropical (Rua Gamboa de Cima 24, Centro, tel. 71/3487-1213, www.boatetropical.com, 11pm-6am Fri.-Sat., cover R$10-20) is the third and latest incarnation of a gay club called Holmes whose nocturnal happenings were legendary throughout Brazil in the 1980s. The decor is festive, gaudy, and heavy on Carmen Miranda tributes. There are two bars, a lounge, the requisite dance floor, and a stage where local drag queens entertain the mixed yet largely gay audience.

Opened in 2013, Commons Studio Bar (Rua Odilon Santos 224, Rio Vermelho, www.commons.com.br, tel. 71/3022-5620, 10pm-5am Fri.-Sat. cover R$15-25) has been anointed one of the most scaldingly hot destinations to trip the night fantastic. A mixture of cutting-edge live bands and DJ-hosted *festas* keep the city's young *alternativos* grooving on the wood-paneled dance floor until dawn.

Performing Arts

Salvador is famed for its rich cultural scene, particularly when it comes to music. For major musical, dance, and theatrical events—featuring big-name performers from both Brazil and abroad—check out the offerings at Salvador's Teatro Castro Alves (Campo Grande, tel. 71/3535-0600, www.tca.ba.gov.br), a gleaming modernist theater directly in front of Campo Grande. Don't miss the nightly dance performances given by Balé Folclórico da Bahia, held at the Teatro Miguel Santana (Rua Gregório de Matos 49, Pelourinho, tel. 71/3322-1962, www.balefolcloricodabahia.com.br, 8pm Mon. and Wed.-Sat., R$40). Although not strictly "folkloric," the graceful and acrobatic choreographies are inspired by capoeira, Candomblé, and many other Afro-Bahian traditions, and the dancers themselves are breathtakingly fluid.

Festivals and Events

Salvador has all the prerequisite ingredients for a good party: an idyllic climate, a powerful musical and cultural heritage, the mix of Catholic and Candomblé, and a population that loves an excuse to take to the streets and display their *ginga* (graceful moves).

★ CARNAVAL

Billed as the biggest street party on the planet (it's listed in *Guinness Book of World Records* as such), Salvador's Carnaval lures an estimated 2 million local and international revelers to the streets of the Centro, Barra, and Ondina for madness, mayhem, and plenty of dancing.

Carnaval begins on a Thursday in February or early March (it's the week prior to Lent; the date changes every year according to the Catholic calendar). The merrymaking gets underway timidly (although in Salvador, "timid" is very relative) on Thursday night, when keys to the city are handed over to the Rei Momo (Carnaval King). It then continues until noon on Ash Wednesday, when the leader of the Timbalada *bloco,* Carlinhos Brown, leads a procession of *trios elétricos*—massive stages on wheels outfitted with mega speakers (as well as dressing rooms, lounges, bars, and restrooms)—along Avenida Oceânica. The stages propel Carnaval's major musical artists and their guests around the 25 kilometers (16 mi) of closed-off thoroughfares. Each *trio* belongs to a *bloco*, a type of closed club, which is literally cordoned off from the masses on the sidewalks. For a fee (ranging R$300-3,000, payable at Central do Carnaval stands), you can join a *bloco*. You'll get a festive costume (known as an *abadá*), unlimited beverages, use of the toilet, and protection, courtesy of the *cordeiros*, who are (very poorly paid) to (wo)man the ropes separating *blocos* from the rest of the populace, known as the *pipoca* ("popcorn").

Although being part of a *bloco* allows you to be right in the center of things, you can also leave your valuables at home and take to the streets. This will give you a chance to wander around more freely and fully experience the variety of offerings. There are many *blocos*: indigenous, African—such as Olodum (tel. 71/3321-5010, www.olodum.com.br) and Ilê Aiyê (tel. 71/2103-3400, www.ileaiyeoficial.com)—and transvestite. *Afoxés*, such as Filhos de Gandhy (tel. 71/3321-7073, www.filhosdegandhy.com.br), whose all-male members dress in long white robes and turbans, are religiously oriented. There are even hip-hop and reggae groups and DJ-led raves.

Carnaval unfolds in three areas, known as "circuits." While the Dôdo Circuito in Barra and Ondina tends to attract the big names associated with *axé* music (Bahia's signature style of throbbing commercial pop), the Osmar Circuito between Campo Grande and Praça Castro Alves features the more traditional and less commercial *blocos*. The Circuito Batatinha in the Pelourinho, with its small samba groups and marching bands, is perfect for children and families.

Whether you indulge for one night or all six, as an unadulterated sensory hedonistic experience, Salvador's Carnaval is beyond comparison. If you can't take the heat (or the blaring music and chaotic crowds), get out of the city. But if you're in the mood to dance, sing, *pular* (jump up and down), and *paquerar* (flirt) from dusk till dawn and back again, you'll be absolutely thrilled.

Considering the possible mayhem when you throw a couple of million drunken people together in 35°C (95°F) heat, Carnaval is surprisingly peaceful, thanks to heavy police presence. That said, it's best to use caution. Certainly, don't party alone. Pickpockets abound. Be smart and carry photocopied documents and just enough money for snacks, beers, and a cab ride.

For more information about joining a *bloco*, contact Central do Carnaval (tel. 71/3535-7000, www.centraldocarnaval.com.br). For information about Carnaval, check out www.carnaval.salvador.ba.gov.br.

FESTA DOIS DE JULHO

While the rest of Brazil celebrates independence on September 7, for Bahians independence is all about July 2, when courageous local forces expelled Portuguese troops from Bahian soil. The festivities begin on the morning of July 2, with a procession from the Igreja of Lapinha through the historic center and the Pelourinho, then finishing up in the afternoon at Campo Grande. Politicians of all parties show up, as do traditional marching bands and baton twirlers, but the quasi-mystical Caboclo figures, effigies of mixed indigenous and European race that are carried through the streets in ornate chariots, are the main draw.

FESTA DE SANTA BÁRBARA

One of the most moving celebrations is held on December 4 in honor of the patron saint of markets and firefighters, Santa Bárbara. Due to her association with the fiery and feisty Iansã, devotees, in large part women (including many transsexuals), dress in red and white, the symbolic colors of the *orixá*. There's a mass in front of the Igreja de Nossa Senhora do Rosário dos Pretos in the Largo do Pelourinho, then a procession passes through the historic center, stopping at the main fire station and the Mercado de Santa Bárbara, where free *caruru* (made from more than 5,000 okra) is distributed. Throughout the day and into the night, the streets resemble a dancing sea of red.

FESTA SENHOR DOS NAVEGANTES
In Salvador, New Year's Day is synonymous with this beautiful celebration in which the effigy of Nosso Senhor dos Navegantes is transported around the Bay of All Saints by a fleet of decorated boats. From Praia da Boa Viagem, religious music and lots of samba accompany landlubbers watching the procession.

LAVAGEM DO BONFIM
The most important religious and popular *festa* on the calendar takes place on the second Thursday in January. Dressed in traditional white garb and strings of beads, Bahianas lead an 8-kilometer (5-mi) procession of similarly white-attired and perfumed devotees and partyers from Comércio to the Igreja de Bonfim for the washing (*lavagem*) of the church steps. The *festa* honors Senhor do Bonfim (associated with the important *orixá* Oxalá, whose color is white). After the crowd is doused with blessed water and perfume, the party really gets going, lasting long into the night.

FESTA DE IEMENJÁ
As the sun rises on February 2, Candomblé worshippers and Bahians from all walks of life begin arriving at the Casa do Peso in Rio Vermelho, where they leave offerings of flowers and perfumes for Iemenjá, the beloved queen of the seas. At the end of the afternoon—when the presents are transported by a fleet of hundreds of decorated fishing boats and tossed into the sea—the streets of Rio Vermelho erupt in major partying.

SHOPPING
Salvador isn't a big shopping mecca. The Mercado Modelo (Praça Visconde de Cairu 250, tel. 71/3241-2849, 9am-7pm Mon.-Sat., 9am-2pm Sun.) sells Bahian trinkets and

souvenirs, jewelry, and handicrafts. The city's oldest and biggest daily outdoor *mercado* is Feira de São Joaquim (in Calçada), best for authentic Candomblé artifacts. Most purchases are concentrated in the Pelourinho and Barra. The Pelô has an assortment of boutiques and galleries (and tourist traps).

Didara (Rua Gregório de Matos 20, Pelourinho, tel. 71/3321-9428, www.didara.com.br, 10am-6pm Mon.-Sat.) is the boutique of clothing and housewares designer Goya Lopes. After studying the history of African textiles, Lopes began making clothes for local musicians. Over time, her designs—sold under the name Didara, which means "good" in Yoruba—have attracted an international following who seek out her bold and colorful yet refined clothing and housewares inspired by African design motifs.

Another homegrown talent who has made a mark on the national fashion scene is Márcia Ganem (Rua das Laranjeiras 10, Pelourinho, tel. 71/3322-2423, www.marciaganem.com.br, 9am-7pm Mon.-Sat.). Her contemporary designs for women are mostly made of polyamide fibers recycled from rubber tires—a surprisingly delicate material that has become her trademark. Equally original is her line of jewelry. Natural fibers derived from regional palms (such as piaçava and ouricuri) inspire Marta Muniz (Rua João de Deus 17, Pelourinho, tel. 71/3321-4728, www.lojamartamuniz.blogspot.com.br, 11am-8pm Mon.-Sat.) to weave tropically textured eco-housewares and decorative objects.

Few CD stores remain in the city, yet Cana Brava Records (Rua João de Deus 22, tel. 71/3321-0536, www.canabrava.org, 9am-close Mon.-Sat.), run by a knowledgeable American expat, is a great place to listen to and purchase Brazilian music. Among its offerings, Cana Brava specializes in traditional music of the Bahian Reconcâvo region.

Cultuarte (Rua das Laranjeiras 48, tel. 71/3495-1736, www.cultuartebahia.com, 9:30am-5:30pm Mon.-Fri.), in the Pelô, is an association of local artists and artisans who earn their living by creating compellingly original clothing, accessories, and decorative objects that draw upon and seek to strengthen Afro-Bahian culture. For art, housewares, and handicrafts made by artists from all over the state of Bahia, a great source is the Instituto de Artesanato Visconde de Mauá (Rua Gregório de Matos 27, tel. 71/3116-6712, www.maua.ba.gov.br, 9am-6pm Mon.-Fri., 9am-2pm Sat.). Although pricy, the quality of the work is high. There is a second boutique at Porto da Barra (tel. 71/3116-6190, 9am-6pm Mon.-Sat.). Also in Barra is Salvador's largest centrally located shopping mall. Just off the Praia do Farol, Shopping Barra (Av. Centenário 2992, Barra, tel. 71/3264-7128, www.shoppingbarra.com, 10am-10pm Mon.-Sat., 3pm-9pm Sun.) offers three gloriously air-conditioned levels featuring Brazilian designer boutiques, food courts, bookstores, and a cineplex.

ACCOMMODATIONS

Where you decide to stay in Salvador depends on your priorities and personal taste. To soak up lots of colonial atmosphere, the Pelourinho and neighboring *bairro* of Santo Antônio offer all sorts of options, from backpacker-filled hostels to sophisticated boutique hotels in restored 17th- and 18th-century mansions. Beach bunnies will prefer to be in Barra (still very central) or at the more traditional hotel chains in Ondina and Rio Vermelho. Though other options exist farther along Salvador's coast, particularly in Itapuã, their distance from the center and lack of neighborhood attractions make them impractical.

Pelourinho and Santo Antônio

The Pelourinho is always humming (or drumming) with activity. It can also be noisy and touristy. Off the beaten path and only reachable by taxi or on foot—factor in a steep climb up the Ladeira do Carmo—are the many *pousadas* in tranquil Santo Antônio, where many foreigners have purchased and converted 18th- and 19th-century houses into stylishly, intimate lodgings.

R$50-200

Occupying a biscuit-colored colonial mansion, the well-run and air-conditioned Hostel Galeria 13 (Rua da Ordem Terceira 23, Pelourinho tel. 71/3266-5609, www.hostelgaleria13.com, R$100-140 d, R$32-38 pp) functions as the unofficial headquarters for the young and the sleepless (it's not exactly quiet). Compensating for the lack of cooking facilities are a tapas bar, pool, Moroccan lounge, free happy hour caipis, and breakfast until noon.

Tucked away on a tranquil residential street, Pousada Baluarte (Ladeira do Baluarte 13, Santo Antônio, tel. 71/3327-0367, www.pousadabaluarte.com., R$140-180 d) is a welcoming and flawlessly run Bahian B&B with a quintet of small but cozy rooms. Charming owner Zelina doles out everything from homemade breakfasts to insider tips.

R$200-400

With a great location near the Terreiro de Jesus, the French-owned Casa do Amarelindo (Rua das Portas do Carmo 6, tel. 71/3266-8550, www.casadoamarelindo.com, R$350-530 d) offers 10 elegant and spacious guest rooms in a 19th-century mansion. Don't worry about noise; windows and doors are insulated from the bustle outside, ceiling fans and mini fridges are equipped with silencers, and kids under 14 aren't allowed. The swimming pool and rooftop lounge, as well as most guest rooms, boast wonderful views of the surrounding baroque architecture and the Bay of All Saints. A small gym offers morning capoeira classes, and there is an innovative restaurant on site.

On Rua Direita de Santo Antônio, you will find a handful of attractive *pousadas* located in colonial mansions. Many have terraces with sweeping views of the Baía de Todos os Santos, and charming bars where you can have a drink should you decide not to check in. Owners and staff are invariably multilingual. Pousada Colonial (Rua Direita de Santo Antônio 368, Santo Antônio, tel. 71/3243-3329, www.colonialpousada.com, R$190-280

d) offers good value. Large, spotless guest rooms come in a variety of prices and sizes. The top floor suite, with a private balcony and splendid views, is marvelous.

Pousada do Pilar (Rua Direita de Santo Antônio 24, Santo Antônio, tel. 71/3241-2033, www.pousadadopilar.com, R$260-430 d) is a particularly pleasant option. The 12 immense guest rooms are handsomely furnished and flooded with natural light. Only seven have sea views, but everyone can partake of the lavish breakfast served on the panoramic terrace overlooking the bay.

Owned by an English artist with a penchant for red fish (all the wooden furnishings are decorated with bright scarlet fish swimming against a sea-blue background) Pousada Redfish (Rua Direita de Santo Antônio 442, Santo Antônio, tel. 71/3241-0639, www.hotelredfish.com, R$220-350 d) inhabits a vast, beautifully renovated colonial building beside the 18th-century Igreja Nossa Senhora de Boqueirão. Exterior and interior have been painted in watery shades of green; guest rooms—both standard and the luxury suites—are clean, cool, and quite sizable (the largest ones easily sleep six).

R$400-600

The Pestana Convento do Carmo (Rua do Carmo 1, tel. 71/3327-8400, www.pestana.com/br, R$490-820 d) occupies a 16th-century convent that, aside from some discreet and very handsome trappings of luxury, is remarkably faithful to its religious roots. Cells that once housed Carmelite nuns have been converted into 80 tasteful (if rather neutral) guest rooms. Arcaded cloisters shelter a bar and Portuguese restaurant that face a profusion of tropical plants and a swimming pool. Amenities include a library, L'Occitane spa, fitness center, theater, and, of course, chapel.

OVER R$600

Housed in two 17th-century colonial mansions that overlook the Largo de Cruzeiro São Francisco, the French-owned Hotel Villa Bahia (Largo de Cruzeiro São Francisco 16/18, Pelourinho, tel. 71/3322-4271, www.lavillabahia.com, R$530-730 d) pays heavy homage to both Brazil's and Portugal's past. Each of the 17 luxurious guest rooms is inspired by former colonies ranging from Macau to Madagascar. Colonial antiques abound, as do baroque accessories, jacaranda, and Portuguese ceramic tiles (even the staff wears period getups). Inner courtyards and a pool offer respite from the hustle and bustle outside. The on-site restaurant serves fresh local produce with a marvelously French twist.

★ Hotel Aram Yami (Rua Direita de Santo Antônio 132, Santo Antônio tel. 71/3242-9412, www.hotelaramyami.com, R$520-900 d), whose name is Tupi for "sun and night," alludes to the trouble you'll have *not* spending 24 hours a day here. A Brazilian-Spanish couple, both architects, purchased this colonial mansion as a second home and then decided it was too large to keep to themselves. Now this seductive hotel offers five roomy apartments, each a private oasis; restored colonial features fuse harmoniously with contemporary furnishings, while Bahian *artesanato* mingles with Chinese silk pillows and jewel-hued Japanese lanterns. Two swimming pools (one belongs to the two-bedroom master suite), a bewitching bar, and multiple verandas with sea views are further conducive to an utter sense of well-being.

Barra

Barra has tons of accommodations. Apart from the soulless chain hotels, a few enterprising souls are converting the neighborhood's surviving villas, tucked away in tranquil residential streets, into appealing B&Bs and *pousadas*.

R$50-200

Santeria Hostel Bar (Av. Sete de Setembro 2914, tel. 71/3012-7030, www.santeriahostel-bar.com.br, R$120-150 d) occupies a renovated three-story house perched at the top of Ladeira da Barra; offsetting the steep climb up from the beach is the sunset over the Bay of All Saints gleaned from the lounge/terrace.

A Frida Kahlo color scheme, accessorized by popular Bahian saints and *orixás*, brightens up the two small dorm rooms (R$50 pp) and three doubles.

A pretty tree-lined residential street, Rua Afonso Celso has dozens of still-surviving villas, and a handful have been converted into *pousadas*. Âmbar Pousada (Rua Afonso Celso 485, tel. 71/3264-6956, www.ambar-pousada.com.br, R$140-160 d, R$43-53 pp) is a mixture of *pousada* and hostel that prides itself on its familial atmosphere. Staff are gracious and helpful, and the homey common rooms and verandas are conducive to hammock-swinging, journal-writing, Web surfing, and checking out the next day's itinerary (or lack thereof) in your guidebook. The guest rooms (located off the courtyard) are well maintained and feature portable boom boxes for sampling the eclectic CD collection. Be sure to visit the bar, where you can get a mean caipirinha.

Only a block from the beach is the low-key and attractive Pousada Estrela do Mar (Rua Afonso Celso 119, tel. 71/3264-4882, www.estreladomarsalvador.com, R$150-225 d). The friendly Scottish owners have transformed two houses into nine apartments (the upstairs ones are nicer), decorated in maritime-inspired shades of blue and white. A laid-back vibe reigns. Pousada Noa Noa (Av. Sete de Setembro 4295, tel. 71/3264-1148, www.pousadanoanoa.com, R$160-200 d) has a privileged beachfront location in a hibiscus-colored mansion next to Barra's lighthouse. Its 12 guest rooms—named after 12 European (mostly French) artists—are simple but nicely finished and accessorized. If you can't get one with ocean views, toast your "bad" luck by adjourning to the terrace bar, which, libations aside, is an idyllic spot to watch the sunset. Be forewarned that during Carnaval and New Year's, the place will be one big *festa*.

R$200-400

The brother-sister team at ★ Casa da Vitória (Rua Aloísio de Carvalho 95, Vitória, tel. 71/3013-2016, www.casadavitoria.com,

R$270-350 d) converted their handsome two-story family residence, on a quiet cul-de-sac off swank Corredor da Vitória, into a casual guesthouse that feels just like home (albeit one with a fabulous collection of artworks by contemporary Bahian artists). Seven pretty and personalized guest rooms feature antique and modern wood furnishings and marble bathroom fixtures; the largest room boasts a private veranda with sea views, while those at the back are a bit dim. Closer to the beach, Casa Petúnia Boutique (Rua Engenheiro Milton Oliveira 217, tel. 71/3264-5458, R$190-325 d) is a terrific B&B-style option that receives raves for the Bahian hospitality of English-speaking hosts Marcos and Petúnia. Seven spotless white and soothing rooms offer modern comfort.

Rio Vermelho

Salvador's top-of-the-line big chain beach hotels are concentrated in the middle-class neighborhoods of Ondina and Rio Vermelho. Rio Vermelho is picturesque and full of transportation options, although not as central as Barra. The beaches are not good for swimming, but the location is perfect for its vibrant nightlife.

R$50-200

Since opening in 2012, F Design Hostel (Travessa Prudente de Moraes 65, tel. 71/3035-9711, www.fdesignhostel.com, R$200-220 d, R$55-65 pp) has been touted as not only the best hostel in Salvador, but in all of Brazil. The brainchild of celebrated Brazilian actor/comic and Salvador-lover Luiz Fernando Guimarães, this uber-cool, gay-friendly hostel treats everything—from bunks to the communal bathrooms—with generous dollops of sophisticated design. There's a film screening room and a rooftop bar with a pool.

R$200-400

Located in a charming pink colonial house overlooking the sea, the Hotel Catharina Paraguaçu (Rua João Gomes 128, tel. 71/3334-0089, www.hotelcatharinaparaguacu.

Acarajé

One of the most distinctive fragrances you'll encounter in Salvador is the scent of *acarajés* sizzling in cauldrons of amber-colored *dendê* (palm oil). Made of pounded black-eyed beans, these round fritters are fluffy on the inside and crunchy on the outside. Once the *acarajé* is cut in half, you have the option of several traditional fillings: dried shrimp, *vatapá* (a puree of bread, shrimp, ginger, coconut milk, and cashews), *caruru* (a puree of diced okra), *salada* (a mixture of chopped tomatoes and cilantro), and spicy *pimenta*. *Acarajé* (along with *abarás*) is the city's favorite snack food. Enjoy it at these favorite Bahianas:

- **Acarajé da Neinha** (Av. Sete de Setembro, Centro, 2:30pm-9pm Mon.-Fri., 10:30am -7pm Sat.) at the entrance to Rua Politeama

- **Acarajé do Gregório** (Av. Centenário 2992, Barra, 2pm-10pm Mon.-Fri., 10am -8pm Sat.) in front of Shopping Barra

- **Dinha** (Largo de Santana, Rio Vermelho, 4:30pm-midnight, Mon.-Fri., noon-midnight Sat.-Sun.)

- **Regina** (Largo de Santana, Rio Vermelho, 3pm-10:30pm Tues.-Fri., 10am-10pm Sat.)

- **Cira** (Largo da Mariquita, Rio Vermelho, 10am-11pm daily), with an original Itapuã location (Rua Aristides Milton, 10am-10pm Tues.-Thurs., 10am-midnight Fri.-Sat.)

com.br, R$210-250 d) is a favorite of both Brazilian and foreign travelers who appreciate the intimate atmosphere. The 32 guest rooms are cozy if not stylish; more alluring are the common spaces and surrounding gardens.

R$400-600

The **Zank Boutique Hotel** (Rua Almirante Barroso 161, tel. 71/3083-4000, www.zank-brasil.com.br, R$350-570 d) offers a Bahian boutique experience with a welcome shot of contemporary. The 16 elegant guest rooms are divided between a 100-year-old villa and a sleek annex with floor-to-ceiling windows. Both buildings share a courtyard garden and overlook the sea. It's worth springing for a room with a view. A spa, lounge, reading room, and rooftop pool compensate for the lack of a nearby beach.

FOOD

A potent mixture of African, Portuguese, and indigenous influences, and with an emphasis on fish and seafood, Bahian cuisine is justly celebrated for its colorful presentations and sophisticated flavors. Palm oil, coconut milk, peppers, cilantro, lime, dried shrimp, and cashews create dishes that are both suave

and piquant, and often as fragrant as they are delicious.

Soteropolitanos are famous nibblers. Many meals are enjoyed communally around a bar table (many bars double as restaurants) or on the beach, and delicacies such as *acarajé* and *cocada* are savored in the street. The largest concentrations of eateries tend to be in tourist areas such as the Pelourinho and Barra as well as in Rio Vermelho.

Pelourinho and Santo Antônio

There is no shortage of restaurants in the Pelourinho. A longtime favorite for Bahian fare that's frequented by locals is **Axego** (Rua João de Deus 1, Pelourinho, tel. 71/3242-7481, noon-10pm daily, R$25-35). The restaurant is hidden on the second floor of an old building and serves excellent *moqueca* and *bobó de camarão* without a lot of fuss. Vital Abreu, the owner of **Ponto Vital** (Rua das Laranjeiras 23, Pelourinho, tel. 71/3215-3225, 11:30am-11:30pm Tues.-Sun., R$20-30), serves exotic dishes from his hometown of Santo Amaro da Purificação (in the Recôncavo). Those eager to try an authentic *feijoada* (innards and all) should grab a seat at the small and simple **Alaíde do Feijão** (Rua 12 de Outubro 2,

Pelourinho, tel. 71/3321-6775, 11:30am-10pm daily). Local institution Alaíde Conceição learned how to make this classic Brazilian bean-and-meat stew from her mother, who sold *feijoada* on the streets of the Cidade Baixa. *Feijoadas* cost R$25 and easily serve two; choose between *mulata* and *preta* (black) versions (which refer to the color of the beans).

The **Restaurante do SENAC** (Largo do Pelourinho 13, Pelourinho, tel. 71/3324-8107, www.ba.senac.br, 11:30am-3:30pm Mon.-Sat., R$40) is a touristy but terrific option for its diversity of Bahian cuisine. The restaurant is located in a spacious colonial mansion and is operated by the Senac restaurant school, so the (somewhat formal) service is extremely attentive. The food is carefully prepared and presented by professors and students—an all-you-can-eat buffet features more than 40 regional dishes. For the less culinarily adventurous, a second per-kilo restaurant on the main floor offers a conventional (non-Bahian) but equally tasty buffet.

La Figa (Rua das Laranjeiras 17, Pelourinho, tel. 71/3322-0066, www.ristorantelafiga.com, noon-midnight Mon.-Sat., noon-6pm Sun., R$25-35) is a laid-back yet stylish Italian eatery whose vibrant owner-chef hails from Padua and makes all his fresh pasta by hand. Other strengths are the seafood dishes and pizzas (served at night). For something lighter, tuck into a salad, sandwich, or pastry at **Cafelier** (Rua do Carmo 50, Santo Antônio, tel. 71/3241-5095, www.cafelier.com.br, 2:30pm-9:30pm Thurs.-Tues., R$10-20), occupying an atmospheric mansion teetering over the Bay of All Saints.

Facing onto the Igreja e Convento de São Francisco, French-owned **Le Glacier Laporte** (Largo do Cruzeiro 21, Pelourinho, tel. 71/3266-3649, 10am-9pm daily) serves wonderful sorbet made from local ingredients that packs a Parisian wallop of distilled flavor.

Cidade Baixa

Almost immediately upon opening in 2005, **Amado** (Av. do Contorno 660, Comércio, tel. 71/3322-3520, noon-midnight Mon.-Sat.,

noon-5pm Sun., www.amadobahia.com.br, R$65-85) was crowned as Salvador's undisputed king of contemporary cuisine. Self-taught Brazilian chef Edinho Engel holds court in a spacious modernist warehouse suspended above the Bay of All Saints, where the ocean fuses perfectly with the restaurant's wood, glass, and jungle of potted plants. Local ingredients—with an emphasis on seafood and fish—receive daring and sophisticated treatment, and the impressive wine cellar features more than 3,000 bottles. Unfortunately, service can be exasperatingly slow.

If you visit the Igreja de Bonfim, take advantage of its proximity to the **Recanto da Lua Cheia** (Rua Rio Negro 66, Monte Serrat, tel. 71/3315-1275, 11am-11pm Wed.-Sat., 11am-5pm Sun., R$20-30). The ocean views are just as mesmerizing (if not more so), but the food, ambiance, and clientele are completely different at this typically Soteropolitano restaurant, whose tables are shaded by a canopy of tropical fruit trees. The house specialty is the *moqueca de peguari,* made with shellfish from the island of Itaparica, famed for its aphrodisiac qualities. There's often live music at night, and things can get slow and cacophonous on weekends. Nearby **Sorveteria da Ribeira** (Praça General Osório 87, Ribeira, tel. 71/3316-5451, www.sorveteriadaribeira.com.br, 9am-10:30pm Mon.-Fri., 9am-midnight Sat.-Sun.) is an ice cream parlor in the pretty seaside neighborhood of Ribeira that has been around since 1931. Local tour buses make the trip out here just so out-of-towners can sample a scoop or two of the 50 homemade flavors, including toasted coconut, guava and cream, tapioca, and tamarind.

Centro

There are lots of cheap eats in the bustling Centro, although not so many good ones. However, several long-standing Soteropolitano institutions—which have been offering up delicious *comida caseira* (home cooking) for decades—are definitely worth your while. Close to the Pelourinho and just off the Praça Castro Alves, **Mini Cacique**

(Rua Ruy Barbosa 29, tel. 71/3243-2419, 11am-3:30pm Mon.-Fri., R$15-30) is a favorite lunch destination for businesspeople, which means it can get a little noisy. The elderly waitresses in pumpkin-colored uniforms are atypically brisk, so you won't have to wait long to dig into the well-seasoned dishes. The daily specials are the cheapest and often the most succulent.

Facing a flower market in the lively neighborhood of Dois de Julho, the small and somewhat claustrophobic Porto do Moreira (Rua Carlos Gomes 486, Dois de Julho, tel. 71/3322-4112, 11:30am-4pm Mon.-Sat., 11am-3pm Sun., R$20-30) is a throwback to Bahia of yesteryear with its tiled walls and whirring fans. If it seems as if the place was ripped from the pages of a Jorge Amado novel, know that Bahia's favorite author was an assiduous fan of the 70-year-old family restaurant's delicious *bacalhaus* (Portuguese salted cod, prepared in various manners) and *moquecas* (including the unusual *moqueca de carne,* made of beef meat seasoned with dried shrimp and palm oil).

A practical and pleasant option for lunch or dinner is the fresh and varied per-kilo buffet at the Teatro Castro Alves's Café Teatro (Rua Leovigildo Figueiras 18, Campo Grande, tel. 71/3328-5818, 11:30am-3pm daily, 5pm-11pm performance nights, R$15-20). Local and visiting musicians, dancers, and thespians performing at Salvador's premiere theater eat here, making it a great place for people-watching.

Barra

Barra has its own share of eating options (and the more obvious tourist traps). For a light and wholesome lunch between bronzing sessions, head over to the jasmine-scented Ramma (Rua Lord Cochrane 76, tel. 71/3264-0044, www.rammacozinhanatural.com.br, 11:30am-3:30pm daily, R$15-25), which serves a healthy yet appetizing per-kilo and largely vegetarian menu with Asian leanings. It's a favorite with Salvador's yoga and Pilates crowd. You'll find a second location

in the Pelourinho (Largo do São Francisco 7, tel. 71/3321-0495, noon-4pm Mon.-Sat.). Another per-kilo favorite that draws a more businesslike crowd is Spaghetti Lilas (Rua Professor Fernando Luz 75, tel. 71/3237-9592, 11:30am-2:30pm Mon.-Fri., noon-4pm Sat.-Sun., R$20-30). Low ceilings and an excess of stucco aside, the decor is cool and clean and the mouthwatering buffet has plenty of appetizing local and international choices to fill up on.

Seemingly just another innocuously laid-back sidewalk *boteco,* La Lupetta (Rua Marquês de Leão 161, tel. 71/3264-0495, 6pm-close Mon.-Sat., noon-11pm Sun., R$20-30) is actually operated by the owner of what was once Salvador's best Italian restaurant. The menu offers very decent Italian fare, from creative antipasti to irresistible pizzas and pastas.

Rio Vermelho

The boho hood of Rio Vermelho comes to life at night with dozens of restaurants where one can drink, and even more bars where one can eat. The rest of the *orla* is less interesting, although a few legendary seafood restaurants make great lunch stops after a morning spent lolling on the beaches between Barra and Itapuã.

Catering to Rio Vermelho's significant vegetarian fringe, Manjeiricão (Rua Fonte de Boi 3B, tel. 71/3565-8305, noon-3pm Mon.-Sat., R$15-25) has a diverse and nicely priced per-kilo buffet and an oasis-like ambiance.

Dona Mariquita (Rua do Meio 178, tel. 71/3334-6947, www.donamariquita.com.br, noon-5pm and 6pm-midnight daily, R$25-40) specializes in "Northeastern recipes in extinction"—that is, the kind of honest grub that used to be found on street corners, marketplaces, and kitchens throughout Brazil's Northeast. The menu is helpfully divided into *pesada* (hardcore heavy dishes) and *levinho* (lighter fare that won't put you in a coma).

Trendy and more upscale (but no less Bahian) Casa de Tereza (Rua Odilon Santos 45, tel. 71/3329-3016, www.casadetereza.com.

br, noon-midnight Mon.-Sat., noon-5pm Sun., R$60-80) is named after, and presided over by, local superchef Tereza Paim. Paim uses sustainable ingredients (fish supplied by Rio Vermelho's fishermen's colony, hand-pressed *dendê* oil) to revisit Bahian classics in surprising and sophisticated ways. Results run from crunchy manioc shrimp bathed in passion fruit nectar and lobster moqueca to tapioca soufflé topped with a champagne-ginger coulis. Exposed wooden beams and brick walls covered with local art create a warm, let's-stay-a-while ambiance.

For a light bite and a strong dose of culture, drop by Ciranda Café (Rua Fonte do Boi 131, tel. 71/3012-3963, www.cirandabahia.com.br, noon-10pm Mon.-Thurs., noon-midnight Fri.-Sat., noon-10pm Sun.), an inviting space that's a combination gallery, café, emporium, and performance space where you can take in an exhibit, listen to live music, buy organic Bahian chocolate (or an organic cotton T-shirt), and have a bite to eat. Reflecting the Australian chef's devotion to slow food, the creative menu takes advantage of fresh local fish and lots of organic fruit and veg.

INFORMATION AND SERVICES

The state tourist office, Bahiatursa (www.bahiatursa.ba.gov.br), has various locations in the Pelourinho (Rua das Laranjeiras 12, tel. 71/3321-2133, 8:30am-9pm daily), at the airport (tel. 71/3204-1244, 7:30am-11pm daily), and in the *rodoviária* (71/3450-3871, 7:30am-9pm daily). Staff are helpful and friendly. There's also a 24-hour tourist hotline with English service (tel. 71/3103-3103). Pick up the free pocket guide *Agenda Cultural Bahia* for monthly events and entertainment listings. The official Bahian tourism website (www.bahia.com.br) is a great resource, but the Portuguese links are more complete than those in English.

There is a Banco do Brasil (Cruzeiro de São Francisco 11) in the Pelourinho. Others are at Shopping Barra, in front of the Mercado Modelo, at Porto da Barra, and at the airport. HSBC has a branch in Barra (Avenida Marquês de Caravelas 355). Citibank has a branch close to the Farol da Barra (Rua Marques de Leão 71).

You'll find post offices at the airport, as well as in Shopping Barra, at Campo Grande (Rua Visconde de São Lourenço 66), and in Pelourinho (Largo do Cruzeiro de São Francisco 20).

For medical emergencies, dial 192 for Pronto Socorro (First Aid). In Barra, there are two conveniently located hospitals: the Hospital Espanhol (Av. Sete de Setembro 4161, Barra, tel. 71/3264-1500, www.hospitalespanhol.com.br) and the Hospital Português (Av. Princesa Isabel 914, Barra tel. 71/3203-5555, www.hportugues.com.br). In the event of a crime, call 190 to reach the police. For crimes involving tourists, you'll have to deal with the special tourist police force (they're the ones patrolling the Pelourinho wearing Polícia Turistica armbands). The Delegacia do Turista (DELTUR) is on the Largo de Cruzeiro do São Francisco (tel. 71/3116-6817).

TRANSPORTATION

Most international travelers arrive in Salvador by air, although if you're traveling from another city in Brazil, you'll either arrive by bus or car. Salvador is also a popular stop for international cruises.

Air

The Aeroporto Deputado Luís Eduardo Magalhães (Dois de Julho) is the city's main airport (tel. 71/3204-1010, www.aeroportosalvador.net). Located inland from Itapuã, in the *bairro* of São Cristovão, it is around 30 kilometers (19 mi) from the city center. A taxi will cost around R$70 (if you bargain hard). There are also *executivo* air-conditioned buses (R$3) that pass along the coast and head to Praça da Sé, and regular municipal buses (R$2.80), which aren't recommended unless you have very little luggage and an awful lot of time (around 90 min.).

Bus

Salvador's long distance bus station, Rodoviária Central (Av. Tancredo Neves, Iguatemi, tel. 71/3616-8300) is across the street from Shopping Iguatemi. From here you can catch buses to destinations throughout Bahia and Brazil. In front of the *rodoviária*, amidst the daunting traffic and chaos, you can grab city buses to all destinations or (more sagely) hail a cab; a trip to the Pelourinho or Barra will cost you around R$40.

The main municipal bus station in Centro is Lapa, but many buses also pass through Campo Grande en route to the rest of the city. Regular municipal buses cost R$2.80, whereas plush, air-conditioned *executivo* buses (which link Praça da Sé, the Atlantic coast, and the airport) are R$3. The final destination is written on the front of the bus, and the main stops are listed on the side near the back door. If in doubt, ask the *cobrador* (who takes money at the back of the bus), since some buses have very circuitous routes. As a rule, don't carry a lot of valuables since robberies are common. However, don't be surprised if a seated passenger offers to take your bags and hold them safely on his or her lap. This is simply a courtesy.

Taxi

At night, bus service dwindles and it's safer to take a cab. Taxi drivers rarely speak English but are friendly. If you want, bargain with them, but before the meter starts running. Major companies include Chame Táxi (tel. 71/3241-8888) and Ligue Táxi (tel. 71/3357-7777).

Car

Driving in Salvador can be a challenge: Soteropolitanos have a penchant for not adhering to rules of the road. That said, for exploring the surrounding region, especially the beautiful north coast, which boasts an excellent (privatized) highway, having a car is a big bonus. Hertz has an airport office (tel. 71/3377-3633), as does Localiza (tel. 71/3377-4227), which has another in Ondina (Av. Oceânica 3057, tel. 71/3173-9292).

City Tours

Privé Tur (tel. 71/3205-1400, www.privetur.com.br) and Tatur (tel. 71/3114-7900, www.tatur.com.br) specialize in city and regional tours in English; rates run R$150-200 pp for a half-day guided tour. Salvador Bus (tel. 71/3356-6245, www.salvadorbus.com.br, R$45), a (rather conspicuous) double-decker bus, will take you to all the city's far-flung sights with briefs stops at landmarks such as the Igreja do Bonfim and the Barra lighthouse, along with 90 minutes at the Mercado Modelo/Pelourinho. Audio guides in English accompany the tour, which lasts four hours. Four buses make the trip over the course of the day, so you can hop off and on with the same ticket.

North of Salvador

ESTRADA DO COCO

The coast north from Salvador to Praia do Forte is known as the Estrada do Coco, or the Coconut Road (in honor of the coastline's abundance of swaying coconut palms). Although increasingly subject to the whims of real estate developers, the alarmingly urbanized villages boast lovely beaches.

Arembepe

Arembepe, 50 kilometers (31 mi) north of Salvador, was a hippie haven in the 1960s. The actual "village" consisted of ingeniously constructed palm-frond cottages set amid sand dunes; it was so swinging that it attracted the likes of Janis Joplin, Mick Jagger, and Roman Polanski. Some hippies still live (without electricity) in the village, making and selling jewelry and macramé and living off shrimp and fish. The placid lagoons attract a mellow crowd smoking reefer in idyllic surroundings. Show up at the end of the afternoon to catch the sunset and moonrise while floating in the warm waters of the Rio Capivara. The town of Arembepe attracts weekending and summering Soteropolitanos and has been filling up with condos. Despite the recent development, the beaches are attractive (especially if you walk far from town itself).

A languid place to while away the hottest hours of the day, Mar Aberto (Largo de São Francisco 43, tel. 71/3624-1257, www.marabertorestaurante.com.br, 11:30am-9pm Mon.-Thurs., 11:30am-11pm Fri.-Sat., noon-7pm Sun., R$45-55) is easily the best and prettiest (and priciest) of Arembepe's beachfront restaurants. For dessert, try *manjar,* a creamy pudding topped with a peppery mango coulis.

TRANSPORTATION
Arembepe is easily reached from Salvador via highway BA-099. Buses leave throughout the day every 30-60 minutes from the main Lapa bus station (final destination Monte Gordo) and the Terminal França near the Cidade Baixa's Mercado Modelo. The trip takes about an hour and costs R$6.

Praia do Forte
The country's first eco-resort in the 1980s (long before the prefix "eco" even existed), Praia do Forte drew international tourists to its beautiful beaches and surrounding natural attractions: a mixture of native Atlantic forest, lagoons, and mangroves. Before you could say "environmental," the sandy main road became a carefully landscaped and paved thoroughfare, Alameda do Sol, flanked by chic bikini-filled boutiques, jewelry shops, *creperias,* cafés, and even a *shopping.* Though tastefully designed, the commercial strip transformed the flavor of the place. Today, Praia do Forte is lovely and lively, but quite touristy—and becoming more developed by the day.

SIGHTS
One reason for the town's success as a thriving eco-resort is the presence of Brazil's acclaimed Projeto Tamar (an abbreviation of the Portuguese phrase for sea turtles, *tartaruga marinha*). Founded in 1980 by the Brazilian Environmental Agency (IBAMA), this nonprofit research organization works to preserve the lives of the giant sea turtles living along Brazil's Atlantic coast, which is home to five out of seven of the world's sea-turtle species. Until recently, many were facing extinction as a result of rampant overfishing and urbanization that destroyed nesting sites. At Praia do Forte, Projeto Tamar's mission is not only to save the turtles (and their eggs, traditionally a staple food for local fisherfolk), but to actively involve the population in their plight in a sustainable manner. This is done both directly (by patrolling the beach at night to move eggs or hatchlings at risk of being harmed), and indirectly (through the increased tourism the project has brought to the region).

Eggs, hatchlings, and turtles of all ages find refuge at Projeto Tamar (Al. do Sol, tel. 71/3676-0321, www.tamar.com.br, 9am-5:30pm daily, R$16), located on the beach just behind the pretty whitewashed Igreja de São Francisco. It's filled with pools and aquariums where you can observe the turtles at various stages of their existence—from cute, tiny hatchlings to gigantic full-grown creatures capable of living to the ripe old age of 200. The center includes bilingual information and a gift shop selling the infamous turtle-themed paraphernalia (all proceeds go to Projeto Tamar). There's also a shady café on the premises.

Praia do Forte is also the headquarters of the Instituto Baleia Jubarte (Av. do Farol, tel. 71/3676-1463, www.baleiajubarte.org.br, noon-6pm Tues.-Sat., R$6), a research station for studying humpback whales. Between July and October, these 40-ton mammals trade the frigid waters of Antarctica for warm currents more conducive to reproductive activities. Portomar (Rua da Aurora 1, tel.

71/3676-0101, www.portomar.com.br, 4 hours, R$155 pp) offers boat excursions that allow you to get a close-up glimpse at these fascinating giants.

Back on land, an important historical landmark is the Castelo Gárcia d'Ávila (tel. 71/9985-3371, www.fgd.org.br, 9am-5pm Tues.-Sun., R$10). Originally a lowly clerk for the Portuguese monarchy, the ambitious Gárcia d'Ávila, as a reward for his services to the crown, received the *capitânia* of Bahia (which back in the 16th century embraced a large portion of the Brazilian Northeast stretching up to Maranhão). Built between 1551 and 1624 on a strategic hilltop overlooking the sea, his castle—now in ruins—is one of the first stone structures and the only medieval-style fortress in Brazil. The recently renovated Capela de Nossa Senhora da Conceição houses a tiny museum. The castle can be reached by walking along a 2.5-kilometer (1.5-mi) stretch of dirt road known as Rua do Castelo that branches off from the entrance to Praia do Forte, or else via rental bike, quadricycle, or taxi.

SPORTS AND RECREATION

Praia do Forte and the surrounding area offer lots of activities. First and foremost are its palm-fringed beaches, which offer the shelter of crescent-shaped coves and natural pools framed by coral reefs. The clear blue waters of Praia do Papa-Gente—a 20-minute walk north—are perfect for snorkeling (masks and fins can be rented at Projeto Tamar). You can also venture into the Reserva de Preservação Ambiental Sapiranga (Linha Verde, tel. 71/3676-1133, 9am-5pm daily, R$10). Located 2 kilometers south of Praia do Forte (enter from the Linha Verde), this nature reserve unites rivers, lagoons, and virgin Atlantic forest inhabited by endangered creatures such as the *mico-estrela-de-tufos-brancos* (miniature white tufted star monkey) and the *preguiça-de-coleira* (a type of sloth). Various trails weave through the brush, and there are plenty of opportunities for bathing in the Rio Pojuca. Young local guides can be hired at the entrance to take you on trails (price depends on the distance; the longest and most difficult trail takes five hours). Aside from hiking, you can explore the park by horse (R$120 pp for 1 hour) or the popular quadricycle (built for two, R$240 for a 2.5-hour excursion). With a canoe, you can paddle around the Lagoa Timeantube, a haven for close to 200 exotic bird species (R$30 for 1.5 hours). For more information,

Praia do Forte

contact **Portomar** (tel. 71/3676-0101, www. portomar.com.br)

ACCOMMODATIONS

Increasingly upscale and Eurocentric, Praia do Forte is not the cheapest place to stay along Bahia's north coast. However, in off-season and during the week, it's possible to find some good discounts.

Praia do Forte Hostel (Rua da Aurora 3, tel. 71/3676-1094, www.albergue.com.br, R$170-220 d, R$45-60 pp) offers clean rooms and facilities, including a kitchen and attractive garden courtyard. It's ideal for budgeting backpackers seeking dorm accommodations (and bikes and surfboards for rent). A few more *reais* will buy a nicer double room, more privacy, and tranquility (noise can be a factor here) in a *pousada*. **Casa Verde Apart** (Rua do Peixe Espada 100, tel. 71/3676-1531, www.praiadoforteapart.com.br, R$180-220 d) is ideal for families and those who want to keep house. Friendly owners/hosts Marcelo and Mirian rent six spotless and ecofriendly apartments that sleep up to four and include kitchens, hammock-strung verandas, and private parking. Fusing affordability and aesthetics, **Pousada Rosa dos Ventos** (Al. da Lua, tel. 71/3676-1271, www.pousadarosadosventos.com, R$210-310 d) offers six charmingly decorated guest rooms, each outfitted with flat-screen TVs and private terraces. Breakfast and a free afternoon tea service show off the virtuosity of the kitchen staff.

More upscale is **Pousada Refúgio da Vila** (Lot. Aldeia dos Pescadores, tel. 71/3676-0114, www.refugiodavila.com.br, R$400-570 d), whose lofty living and dining areas are beautifully designed and decorated to take advantage of the light and vivid colors of the surrounding gardens and pool. Guest rooms are less spectacular but well appointed—too bad some of the balconies overlook more "urbanized" parts of Praia do Forte—but the breakfasts are out of this world. If you feel like splurging, check into the place that put Praia do Forte on the ecotourist map way back in the 1980s: the **Tivoli Eco Resort Praia do Forte** (Av. do Farol, tel. 71/3676-4000, tel. 0800/71-8888, www.tivolihotels.com, R$840-1,615 d). Set amid beautifully groomed gardens—with swimming pools, bars, and lounge chairs and overlooking a crescent-shaped beach—this sprawling resort is hardly intimate, yet it definitely makes you feel spoiled and relaxed. All the bright and spacious guest rooms have ocean views. The prices might seem a bit steep, but they include a welcome drink, breakfast and dinner (the spreads are marvelous), sports and leisure equipment, and lots of activities for both adults and children. The thalassotherapy sessions featuring algae and heated seawater are a big bonus.

FOOD

Among the array of less enthralling and often overpriced eateries along the main drag of Alameda do Sol, **Sabor da Vila** (Al. do Sol 159, tel. 71/3676-1156, 11:30am-midnight daily, R$25-40) offers a diversity of dishes with some well-executed fish and seafood options. Prettier and pricier is **Terreiro da Bahia** (Al. do Sol 188, tel. 71/3676-1754, www.terreirobahia.com.br, noon-11pm Thurs.-Tues., R$50-70), where owner/chef Tereza Paim uses fresh, locally sourced produce to riff on classic Bahian recipes. Results include shrimp in mangaba coulis and coconut rice. A break from Bahian fare, **Tango Café** (Al. do Sol 269, tel. 71/3676-1637, 2pm-11pm Mon.-Fri., 11am-midnight Sat.-Sun., R$10-20) serves empanadas, sandwiches, and delicious desserts. This is one of the few places in Bahia where you can get a real cappuccino.

TRANSPORTATION AND SERVICES

On Alameda do Sol (near the bus stop) are several ATMs that accept international cards. For more information, visit www.praiadoforte.org.br. Buses leave from Terminal da França, in the Cidade Baixa, stopping at Salvador's Rodoviária Central, approximately every hour between 5am and 6pm with the **Expresso Linha Verde** (tel. 71/3460-3636, R$10). The trip takes around 90 minutes along highway BA-099. Informal vans (R$8) offer more frequent service, but prepared to be squished like sardines.

LINHA VERDE

Up the coast from Praia do Forte, the Estrada do Coco morphs into the Linha Verde (Green Line), stretching all the way to Bahia's frontier with the state of Sergipe. With the exception of the megaresort complex of Costa do Sauípe—with its umpteen international hotels surrounded by a fake theme-park likeness of the Pelourinho—the little fishing villages that dot this beautiful stretch of coast are (for the time being) largely untouched by mass tourism.

Imbassaí

Only 10 kilometers (6 mi) past Praia do Forte, this low-key village is a welcome antidote to Praia do Forte. It attracts a mix of locals, families, gays, and a few fashionistas (bikini spreads for Brazilian *Vogue* are often shot here). The main draw is the beach, which straddles a windswept blue Atlantic on one side and the warm Coca-Cola-colored Rio Imbassaí on the other side. The upshot is that you can spend your day alternating between two utterly relaxing watery worlds.

ACCOMMODATIONS AND FOOD

There are quite a range of good *pousadas* and restaurants in Imbassaí. The most charming of the lot is the ★ **Eco Pousada Vilangelim** (Al. dos Angelins, tel. 71/3677-1144, www.vilangelim.com.br, R$320-390 d). Although the cozy bungalow guest rooms are a little snug, you can always hang out in the main dining and lounge areas (children under 12 aren't allowed). Common spaces extend to the wooden decks, where a tiled swimming pool is framed by lush foliage (including namesake *angelim* trees). The food (especially the lavish breakfasts) is excellent, and the staff is terrifically attentive. You'll get a friendly welcome at **Pousada Cajibá** (Al. das Bromélias, tel. 71/3677-1111, www.pousada-cajiba.com.br, R$180-220 d), set amidst an exuberant garden with a pool frequented by *mico* monkeys. Accommodations are in two-story bungalows; those on the second floor look out onto a canopy of fruit trees. **Casa Viola** (Al. dos Cajueiros, tel. 71/3677-1017, casaviola.wix.com, R$160-200 d) combines atmosphere with affordability in six colorful chalets, whose rusticity is offset by well-chosen decor. Delicious homemade breakfasts and a romantic on-site bistro, verdant garden, and tiny pool up the oasis factor.

barracas facing the beach in Imbassaí

For Bahian specialties such as fish, seafood, and *moquecas,* plant yourself beneath the enormous *mangaba* tree that shelters the Santana Restaurante (Rua da Igreja 1, tel. 71/3677-1237, noon-10pm Thurs.-Tues., R$25-40). Aside from the welcome shade, when ripe the tree's *mangabas* yield a succulent nectar (it will make your lips stick together slightly). Also famed for *moquecas* is Vânia (Al. dos Hibiscos, tel. 71/3677-1040, 11:30am-7:30pm Tues.-Sun., R$25-35), located just off the main drag.

At night, what laid-back action there is unfolds on the main street of Rua das Amendoeiras. É Massa (tel. 71/3676-1067, R$15-25) is an Italian restaurant-bar owned by an Argentinean expat; it serves tasty salads, empanadas, and homemade pizzas and pastas and offers free Wi-Fi for those with laptops. Always abuzz with an older crowd is Nega Fulo (Al. das Amendoeiras, tel. 71/3677-1019, 5:30pm-11pm Mon.-Tues. and Thurs., 5:30pm-midnight Fri., 1pm-midnight Sat.-Sun., R$20-35), a romantically lit pizzeria fused with the equally enticing Jerimum Café, which has elaborate drinks and mouthwatering desserts.

TRANSPORTATION
Imbassaí is 10 kilometers (6 mi) north of Praia do Forte along BA-099. Buses leave from Terminal da França, in the Cidade Baixa, stopping at Salvador's Rodoviária Central, hourly between 5am and 6pm with the Expresso Linha Verde (tel. 71/3460-3636, R$14). The trip takes close to two hours along highway BA-099. Informal vans (R$10) offer more frequent service.

Diogo
Diogo, 4 kilometers (2.5 mi) north of Imbassaí, is more bucolic and less visited. Its most "sophisticated" accommodation is the Belgian-owned Too Cool na Bahia (tel. 71/9952-2190, www.toocoolnabahia.com, R$120-200), whose eight simple but comfortable bungalows (with and without air-conditioning) are set in sand dunes and shaded by large fruit trees. It's a 20-minute walk to reach the beach of Santo Antônio, which, aside from a couple of simple

barracas, is inevitably deserted. In the village, Caminho do Rio (tel. 71/9964-4087, 10am-5pm daily, R$15-30) excels at Bahian specialties such as seafood moqueca.

Getting to Diogo is easy; the Expresso Linha Verde buses and vans that stop in front of Imbassaí also stop in front of the BA-099 turn-off to Diogo. From there, it's a 1-km hike to the village; or take one of the *moto-taxis* usually parked at the entrance.

★ Mangue Seco
At the end of the Linha Verde, 70 kilometers (43 mi) north from Sítio do Conde, is the secluded Mangue Seco. Ever since its otherworldly dunescape made a cameo appearance in *Tieta,* a 1989 *novela* based on the Jorge Amado's novel *Tieta do Agreste,* Brazilians have been flocking to this slice of palmy paradise wedged between the Rio Real and the open Atlantic. Aside from the rustic little fishing village, you'll find yourself surrounded by coconut plantations, mangroves, and snowy white sand beaches whose big waves attract surfers. Thankfully, despite its fame, Mangue Seco's remoteness keeps the crowds at bay.

ACCOMMODATIONS AND FOOD
Mangue Seco has a handful of comfortably rustic accommodations. The nicest of all is Eco Pousada O Forte (tel. 75/3455-9039, www.pousadaoforte.com, R$250-310 d), located along the river between town and the beach. The owner, Yves, is a French adventurer (who sailed solo across the Atlantic from France to Salvador) with a flair for decorating as well as running a restaurant (which has the best wine cellar in town). In town, Pousada Fantasias do Agreste (tel. 75/3455-9011, www.pousadafantasiasdoagreste.com.br, R$150-210 d) offers modern guest rooms and a leafy green central courtyard. Overlooking the river, the cheaper and simpler Pousada Suruby (tel. 75/3455-9061, www.pousadasuruby.com.br, R$120-140 d) boasts a breezy veranda hung with hammocks, along with a restaurant that serves delicious fish and seafood dishes. Also good

for deliciously prepared fish and seafood is Frutos do Mar (tel. 75/3455-9049, 7am-9pm daily, R$20-35), which also offers river views. A Mangue Seco specialty is the delicious crab-like *aratú*, which are used to make *moquecas*. On the beach, you'll also encounter *moque-quinhas,* tasty slices of cured fish wrapped in palm leaves and sold by local boys on the beach for R$1. Don't leave town without trying the amazing homemade *doces,* fruit *licores,* and *sorvetes* at ★ Recanto Dona Sula (tel. 75/3455-9008, 8:30am-8:30pm daily), located right on the sandy main square. Sula's daughter, Ana Flora Amado (a relative of novelist Jorge Amado), presides over the most idyllic ice cream parlor—and best ice cream—you'll ever encounter. Sandwiches and light meals are also available.

To really experience Mangue Seco's dunes you need to rent a dune buggy. A standard one-hour tour costs R$70 for up to four people with stops for pictures and to partake in *esqui-bunda* ("butt-skiing"). Sunset is particularly bewitching. You'll find *bugueiros* in the main square.

TRANSPORTATION

Getting to Mangue Seco is a bit tricky: Take a 15-minute ride in a motorboat (R$45 for up to four people or R$3 pp in a larger boat) from Pontal on the Sergipe side of the Rio Real. Expresso Linha Verde (tel. 71/3460-3636) has three daily buses departing at 7am, 11am and 2pm from Salvador to Indiaroba (five hours, R$35)—from there you'll have to take a taxi (R$40) or minibus (20 minutes) to Pontal. If driving, follow SE-368 (continuation of the Linha Verde) to the Pontal turnoff, then drive another 12 kilometers to the town, where you can stash your car (many villagers offer parking in their gardens for R$15 a day). If the tide is high, ask the boatman to take you directly to your *pousada.* If not, you'll have to lug your bags along a sandy trail.

The Recôncavo

Named after the concave-shaped Bay of All Saints, the Reconcâvo refers to the former sugarcane region surrounding Salvador. Once the major purveyor of Bahia's great wealth, the colonial cities of Santo Amaro and Cachoeira were prosperous regional capitals whose prominence is reflected in the impressive array of baroque churches and gracious mansions that line their sleepy cobblestoned streets and squares. Despite a certain air of dilapidation, the towns retain a distinctive charm. The Reconcâvo is also known for its rich cultural traditions, linked to the African heritage of the largely black population descended from the slaves who worked the sugar plantations. Both towns are within a two-hour drive from Salvador and can be easily visited in a day trip. To soak up the region's history and distinctive flavor, consider staying overnight in Cachoeira.

SANTO AMARO

Only 70 kilometers (43 mi) from Salvador, this typical Recôncavo town—the home-town of Brazilian musical sibling superstars Caetano Veloso and Maria Betânia—is attractive and unpretentious. With elegant squares framed by baroque churches and a couple of ruined plantation manors, it's a pleasant place to wander around for a couple of hours if you're on your way to or from Cachoeira. Highlights include the colonial buildings around the Praça da Purificação, among them the 17th-century Igreja Matriz de Nossa Senhora da Purificação, with its Portuguese tiles, and the imposing 18th-century Convento dos Humildes (9am-1pm Tues.-Sun.), at Praça Padre Inácio Teixeira dos Santos Araujo, which houses a small museum of religious art. Don't leave without sampling the *sequilhos,* crisp buttery biscuits made by the nuns at the convent.

Entertainment and Events

Santo Amaro hosts two *festas populares* in the Recôncavo. On January 6 is the Festas dos Reis, during which the town's squares are given over to music and merrymaking. On May 13, Bembé do Mercado celebrates the abolition of slavery in Brazil in 1888. Offerings are given to the *orixá* Iemanjá, and there are plenty of traditional African-inspired songs and *samba-de-roda* dancing.

★ CACHOEIRA

Two hours from Salvador, this atmospheric town on the banks of the languid Rio Paraguaçu is a small treasure trove of colonial architecture that is slowly being restored. Cachoeira is also a center of Afro-Brazilian culture; there are a large number of traditional Candomblé *terreiros* as well as the Irmandade da Boa Morte (Sisterhood of Good Death)—a female religious order created by freed slaves more than 200 years ago. The order's annual Festa da Boa Morte has become a major event, attracting loads of *afro-descendentes* in search of their ancestral roots.

During the 17th and 18th centuries, Cachoeira was one of the wealthiest and most populous cities in the Brazilian colony. Its strategic location upriver from the Paraguaçu's entrance into the Bay of All Saints made it an important crossroads for the riches—particularly the gold mined in the Chapada Diamantina—that were being shipped from the interior down to the coast and off to Portugal. Its fertile soil lured Portuguese colonists to cultivate sugarcane in the surrounding hills and led to the importation of thousands of African slaves who worked the plantations. While the slaves toiled, their rich masters poured money into the embellishment of the thriving town, bequeathing a legacy of fine baroque churches.

By the early 19th century, colonial rule was being increasingly challenged, and as a hotbed of revolt, Cachoeira achieved national prominence. Cachoeirenses led the battle for independence against Portuguese troops. When Brazil subsequently won its independence, it was in Cachoeira that Dom Pedro I chose to be crowned as Brazil's first emperor.

At the end of the 19th century, sugar prices had diminished and slavery had been abolished. Cachoeira and its neighboring town, São Félix (across the river) still prospered due to the cultivation of tobacco (its quality renowned throughout the world), but today tobacco's importance has dwindled. The glory of former times is but a distant memory preserved in the town's rich architectural and cultural heritage.

Sights

You can discover Cachoeira's treasures in a half-day of pleasant wandering around, which can also include a boat trip along the Rio Paraguaçu.

CENTRO

Praça da Aclamação is a grand square lined with impressive edifices. The Casa da Câmara e Cadeia is the town's 17th-century jailhouse and currently functions as its city hall. You can't miss the splendidly baroque Igreja da Ordem Terceira e Convento do Carmo (tel. 75/3425-4853, 9am-5pm daily). The church is richly decorated with Portuguese ceramic tiles, an ornate gold altar, and an exquisitely paneled ceiling. A side gallery features polychrome Christ figures, produced in the Portuguese colony of Macau, whose gory realism is enhanced by a mixture of bovine blood and rubies. Inside, the Museu de Arte Sacra do Recôncavo (R$5) has a collection of religious art and objects. It can be accessed via the cloister of the magnificent convent, which operates as a *pousada* with a restaurant.

Housed in a handsome civic building, the Museu Regional (tel. 75/3425-1123, 8am-noon and 2pm-5pm Mon.-Fri., 8am-noon Sat.-Sun., R$2) has an unassuming collection of 18th- and 19th-century furniture and decorative objects.

A couple of blocks away, on Rua 13 de Maio, is the coral-colored building that is the headquarters of the Irmandade da Boa Morte

(10am-6pm daily, donation suggested). Inside, a small museum displays photographs detailing the sisterhood's history and traditions, including the famous Festa da Boa Morte. From the museum, a steep ascent leads to the Praça da Ajuda, where you'll come face-to-face with the Igreja de Nossa Senhora da Ajuda, a simple stone church built in the 1590s that happens to be Cachoeira's oldest (sadly, it can't be visited). Descending an equally steep alley in the other direction will bring you to Rua Ana Nery, where you can visit the 17th-century Igreja Matriz Nossa Senhora do Rosário, renowned for its wonderful blue-and-white ceramic tile panels.

SÃO FÉLIX

When through wandering around Cachoeira, cross the rickety British-built wooden bridge that leads across the river to the town of São Félix. Aside from some attractive pastel-colored riverfront buildings, the main interest of São Félix is the Centro Cultural Dannemann (Av. Salvador Pinto 29, tel. 75/3438-3716, www.dannemann.com, 8am-5pm Tues.-Sat.), a warehouse that has been converted into a contemporary art center. Apart from temporary shows, the center hosts the prestigious Bienal do Recôncavo in November of even-numbered years. Famed throughout the world for its fine cigars, Dannemann still produces its heavily perfumed smokes on the premises. To catch a glimpse—and a whiff—of the process, make your way to the rear of the building, where women dressed in white sit at ancient wooden tables, rolling cigars as if it were still 1873. Even if you don't inhale yourself, you might want to buy a few to take home as the ultimate gift for the smokers in your life. Also in São Félix is the Museu Casa Hansen (Ladeira dos Milagres, tel. 75/3245-1453, 9am-5pm Tues.-Fri., 9am-1pm Sat., free). This museum is devoted to the expressive woodcuts and paintings of Hansen Bahia, a German engraver who fled Nazi Germany for Cachoeira (changing his last name along the way) and is located in his former home. Hansen's work reflects a strong local woodcarving tradition that you'll notice as you wander around town.

Festivals and Events

Without a doubt, the most famous event in Cachoeira is the three-day Festa de Nossa Senhora da Boa Morte, held every year in August. If you want to stay in Cachoeira, reserve a hotel *months* in advance. Should you miss this unforgettable celebration, try to make the Festa de Nossa Senhora da Ajuda (mid-Nov.), which features the washing of the steps of the Capela de Ajuda as well as plenty of traditional *samba-de-roda* music and dancing.

Accommodations and Food

The most comfortable and atmospheric—and really quite affordable—place to stay in town is the Pousada Convento do Carmo (Praça da Aclamação, tel. 75/3425-1716, R$90-140 d), with 26 guest rooms that are distributed among the town's 18th-century Carmelite convent. Ceilings are cathedral-high, dark wood is in abundance, and the plain decor is bereft of worldly goods. Slightly more hedonistic are the outdoor pool and an elegant restaurant. It serves a mean *maniçoba*, a heady local stew invented by slaves; the main ingredients include sun-dried beef and pork as well as stewed manioc leaves that must be boiled for three days beforehand to expel their natural toxins. For appetizing home-cooked Bahian fare, head to Beira-Rio (Rua Manuel Paulo Filho 19, tel. 75/3425-5050, 9am-11pm daily, R$10-20), a simple place whose outdoor tables and chairs overlook the river.

Transportation

Santana (tel. 71/3450-4951) provides hourly bus service between Cachoeira and Salvador (R$20) via Santo Amaro, with departures from Salvador's *rodoviária*. If you're driving, take BR-324 from Salvador for 60 kilometers (37 mi) until it meets BA-026 near Santo Amaro. From Santo Amaro, follow BA-026 for 38 kilometers (24 mi) to Cachoeira.

Candomblé Rituals

African slaves who arrived in Bahia came armed with the divinities of their homeland. After Portuguese slave masters banned practices that strayed from Catholicism, many slaves pretended to adopt Christian dogmas and rituals. In reality, they merged Catholic symbols with age-old beliefs preserved from their religious heritages. The result was the syncretic Afro-Brazilian religion known as **Candomblé**.

As Candomblé developed, the *orixás* (traditional African divinities representing various natural forces) became associated with Catholic saints: Oxalá the Creator with Jesus Christ; Iemenjá queen of the seas with Nossa Senhora da Conceição (Our Lady of Conception); Ogum, the great warrior and blacksmith, with both Santo Antônio and São Jorge; and Iansã, goddess of fire and thunderbolts, with Santa Bárbara.

This clever strategy ensured Candomblé's survival for more than four centuries. Still it was brutally repressed, not only by clerical authorities but by the ruling elite. In fact, to this day, there is a lingering prejudice against worshippers, who were known derogatorily as *macumbeiros* (practitioners of *macumba*, or witchcraft).

Terreiros are sacred casas (houses) where rituals and celebrations take place; these are presided over by *mães* and *pais de santos* (venerated Candomblé priests and priestesses). Among the most famous and traditional *terreiros* are Gantois, Ilê Axê Opô Afonja, and Casa Branca.

Although visitors are welcome, Candomblé rituals are sacred events. If you go, dress simply but formally (long pants and shoes for men, a long skirt and modest top for women), inquire beforehand about using a camera, and never join the dance. Candomblé festivities take place on the specific days associated with various *orixás*. The majority of *terreiros* are located in poor suburbs best reached by taxi:

- **Gantois** (Rua Alto do Gantois 23, Federação, tel. 71/3321-9231): Founded in 1849, the most important *festa* is held in honor of Oxossi (June 19).

- **Ilê Axé Opô Afonja** (Rua Direita de São Gonçalo do Retiro 557, Cabula, tel. 71/3384-3321): This traditional *terreiro* houses various *casas*, each devoted to a specific *orixá*. The most important *festas* take place in June-July and September-October.

- **Casa Branca** (Avenida Vasco da Gama 463, Vasco da Gama, tel. 71/3335-3100): Brazil's oldest surviving *terreiro* (dating from 1830) is recognized as a National Cultural Heritage. The most significant *festas*, held in honor of Oxossi and Xango, take place in May-June.

- **Irmandade da Boa Morte** (Sisterhood of Good Death): A religious order founded in the early 19th century by elderly black women of Cachoeira, the sisterhood has become a symbol of Brazilians' black heritage and culture. Members must be women, black, and at least 60 years old (the oldest *irmã* is over 100). The most important festival is the three-day **Festa de Nossa Senhora da Boa Morte** (Aug. 13-15) in honor of the Virgin Mary.

Chapada Diamantina

Due west from Salvador, the dry and dusty landscape of the northeastern Sertão region segues to mountains, and the vegetation turns surprisingly lush, with an abundance of orchids and bromeliads. The transformation signals the beginning of the Chapada Diamantina (Diamond Plateau), a vast and ancient geological region filled with canyons and gorges and crisscrossed by rivers and waterfalls, whose spectacular beauty has made it the No. 1 ecotourist destination in Brazil. Much of this unique and spectacular area is preserved as a national park. If you find yourself in Salvador with three days or more to spare, visiting the Chapada Diamantina is an adventure you won't regret.

★ PARQUE NACIONAL DA CHAPADA DIAMANTINA

The Parque Nacional da Chapada Diamantina is one of the most gorgeous natural regions in Brazil. Within its borders is the Cachoeira da Fumaça, the highest waterfall (380 meters/1,250 feet) in Brazil and the fifth highest in the world, as well as Pico dos Barbados (2,000 meters/6,560 feet), the highest peak in Bahia. Grottoes hide lagoons whose waters turn to piercing blue when touched by the sun. The striking vegetation ranges from giant ferns to the rarest of orchids—and there is always the chance of stumbling on a tiny nugget of gold or a diamond in the rough.

Only one paved road cuts through the 152-square-kilometer (59-square-mi) park, and there is no official entrance. The Chapada can be visited year-round; in summer, the sun can be scorching hot and rain (sometimes lasting for several days) can put a damper on hiking plans. In winter, cooler temperatures (which can become downright chilly at night) coincide with the dry season (Mar.-Oct.), when waterfalls can thin and even dry up.

One of the main bases for exploring the area is Lençóis, a former diamond-mining town now occupied by a lively mix of locals and ecotourists. Mucugê, Andaraí, and Vale do Capão are equally enticing diamond towns offering their own access to several of the park's natural attractions, and their surrounding areas are also worth exploring.

Hiking

The trails that cut through the valleys, plateaus, and canyons of the Parque Nacional da Chapada Diamantina make for some of the most spectacular hiking in Brazil. There are plenty of trails of varying difficulty; many were carved out of the landscape by slaves and gold and diamond miners in the 19th century. These are best traveled with a guide or on an excursion, since many are unmarked. Hire a guide directly via your hotel or through the local Associação de Condutores de

Chapada Diamantina

Gruta Azul
Gruta da Torrinha
Poço do Diabo
Lapa Doce
MORRO DO PAI INÁCIO
BR 24
To Salvador
Tanquinho
Gruta do Lapão
CACHOEIRA PRIMAVERA
Lençóis
RA 142
Palmeiras
CACHOEIRA DA FUMAÇA
Caeté Açu
CACHOEIRA DO SOSSEGO
Vale do Capão
Barra
Rio Roncador
Marimbus Wetlands
PARQUE NACIONAL DA CHAPADA DIAMANTINA
CACHOEIRA DO RAMALHO
Guiné
Andaraí
Poço Azul
Igatu
Poço Encantado
Mucugê
Rio Santo Antônio
Rio São José
Rio Baiano
Rio Preto

© AVALON TRAVEL   SCALE NOT AVAILABLE

Visitante (ACV). The guide association is based in the region's main towns and offers a cheaper option, ideal for those who want a personalized, customized hiking tour. Guided tours cost R$80 (up to four people); overnight trips cost R$150-200 per day (up to six people), which includes food and lodgings. Specialized excursions include transportation and are the way to go for those short on time. Most full-day excursions cost R$130-170 and include transportation, entrance fees, and snacks; optional activities are extra.

LENÇÓIS

Lençóis means "sheets" in Portuguese. The name alludes to the town's early 19th-century origins as a camp for thousands of avid diamond and gold miners, who slept beneath

Parque Nacional da Chapada Diamantina

hall), and the Subconsulado Francês, the former French consulate building. Capela de Santa Luzia (Morro Alto da Tomba, tel. 75/3425-4853, 8am-noon and 2pm-5pm Mon.-Sat., 9am-1pm Sun.) is a small chapel whose interior became a minor work of contemporary art when internationally renowned São Paulo graffiti artist Stephan Doitschinoff decorated the walls with vivid frescos of saints (look for other "interventions" by the artist around town).

Sports and Recreation

Lençóis is close to many of the Chapada Diamantina's most popular sights. One great walk is to follow the Rio Lençóis. After 15 minutes, you'll find yourself at the Poço Serrano, a series of freshwater pools where you can dip your toes or swim and enjoy a panoramic view of the town. Another 15 minutes brings you to the Salão de Areias Coloridas, an area with caves carpeted in multicolored sands sought after by local artists, who layer them in bottles and sell them to tourists. Hire a local youth as a guide (your hotel can do so) to take you to these attractions and to the nearby Cachoeirinha and Cachoeira da Primavera, two small waterfalls where you can swim.

Heading out of town to the southwest (follow the signs), a marked 4-kilometer (2.5-mi) trail leads to the Escorregadeira, a natural rock waterslide that sends you careening down into swimming pools (wear shorts to avoid scraping the skin off your bottom). If you keep going (with a guide, since access is tricky), the trail gets more difficult and involves serious rock climbing. After 8 kilometers (5 mi), you'll reach the impressive Cachoeira do Sossego waterfall, with rock ledges from which you can dive into a deep pool.

A challenging 5-kilometer (3-mi) trek (guide recommended) north from Lençóis brings you to the fantastic Gruta do Lapão, considered to be the largest sandstone cave in South America.

Having a car or being part of an organized

makeshift tents of white cotton fabric after long days combing the region's river in search of precious stones. Although many struck it rich, by the end of the 19th century most of the big rocks had been found. Over the next 100 years, the former boomtown was abandoned and its population shrank significantly. Lençóis's fortunes only revived in 1985, with the creation of the Chapada Diamantina National Park. Despite its size and relative isolation, Lençóis possesses a surprisingly cosmopolitan flavor due to the collection of nature lovers, adventure-sports enthusiasts, and New Age groupies who linger in its cobblestoned streets.

Sights

Tourism has been a catalyst for the ongoing renovation of Lençóis's 19th-century homes and civic buildings, which number more than 200. Among the most splendid traces of its former grandeur are the Igreja Nossa Senhora do Rosário, the wealthy home of the Sá family, which later became the Prefeitura (city excursion is necessary to discover some of the more far-flung and dramatic natural highlights of the Chapada. The Poço do Diabo (Devil's Well), 20 kilometers (12.5 mi) from Lençóis, consists of a series of swimming pools crowned by a majestic 25-meter (82-foot) waterfall. Only 30 kilometers (19 mi) away is Morro do Pai Inácio, a striking 300-meter-high (980-foot) mesa formation. From its cacti-covered summit, you are treated to amazing 360-degree views of the countryside. According to local legend, Inácio was a fugitive slave who scaled the great rock in search of refuge. When cornered by his pursuers, he jumped from the top. Miraculously, he was saved from a fatal fall by the umbrella he opened in midflight. If you can, make the trip in the late afternoon—the sunset viewed from the top is a sight to behold.

Heading west in the direction of Seabra from Lençóis are a number of caverns, all clustered close together. The truly spectacular Gruta da Torrinha (Estrada da Bandeira Km 64, 1-2-hour guided tour R$35 pp) and cavernous Gruta da Lapa Doce (Estrada da Bandeira Km 68, 90-minute guided tour R$20 pp) boast surreally sculptural ensembles of stalactites and stalagmites. Located within walking distance from each other on the Fazenda Pratinha are the Gruta da Pratinha and Gruta Azul (Estrada da Bandeira Km 75, R$20 pp). The latter more than lives up to its name: When lit up directly by the sun (2:30pm-3:30pm daily, Apr.-Sept.), the lagoon at its bottom glows an unearthly azure. At Pratinha, you can rent a flashlight and snorkeling gear (R$20) and plunge right into the clear waters, which are inhabited by 24 species of fish.

Festivals and Events

The two biggest events in Lençóis take place in the winter. Throughout most of mid-late June, the town gets into the swing of things with the typically northeastern Festas Juninas. The feverish high point is the Festa de São João (June 23-24). Expect lots of corn-based delicacies, homemade fruit liqueurs, smoking bonfires, processions, and *forró* music. In August, the town resembles a latter-day Woodstock when it hosts the Festival de Inverno de Lençóis, a musical festival that lures some of the biggest names in Brazilian popular music. January 23 marks the beginning of the Festa de Senhor dos Passos, whose week-long festivities pay homage to the patron saint of miners.

Accommodations

Lençóis has a wide variety of accommodations, and given its backpacking ethos, there is no shortage of cheap lodgings. Simple and downright affordable, the small but quaint Hostel Chapada (Rua Urbano Duarte 121, tel. 75/3334-1497, www.hostelchapada.com.br, R$115-155 d, R$45-55 pp), located in a 19th-century house, has only seven rooms and 27 beds, but lots of greenery, swinging hammocks, and laundry facilities—everything a backpacker dreams of. Budget travelers will also feel at home at the welcoming Pousada da Lua Cristal (Rua dos Patriotas 27, tel. 75/3334-1658, www.pousadaluadecristal.com. br, R$120-130 d), a colonial house with modest but fetching rooms ranging from singles to quintuplets (bathrooms are shared). The great value is enhanced by attentive service and copious breakfasts. Unusual and alluring, Alcino Atelier Estalagem (Rua Tomba Surrão 139, tel. 75/3334-1171, www.alcinoestalagem.com, R$190-290 d) occupies a lovingly restored old house. Owner/artist Alcino Caetano makes guests feel right at home with cozy guest rooms decorated with antiques, glazed tiles, and shards of ceramic painted by local artists. Verandas with hammocks, a garden with fruit trees, and lavish homemade breakfasts, featuring exotica such as taioba quiche, complete the picture.

Ingeniously integrated into its natural surroundings is the ★ Canto das Águas (Av. Senhor dos Passos 1, tel. 75/3334-1154, www. lencois.com.br, R$370-630 d). A river literally runs through the property, providing the gardens, pool, café and celebrated Azul restaurant (open to the public for lunch and dinner) with a constantly soothing soundtrack. More intimate and affordable is the holistic and harmonious **Pousada Vila Serrano Pousada** (Alto do Bomfim 8, tel. 75/3334-1486, www.vilaserrano.com.br, R$190-260 d). Occupying a faux-colonial manse, its nine highly sustainable apartments, designed according to the rules of feng shui, emphasize natural textures, soft lighting, and a fusion between indoor and outdoor environments.

Food

Considering the global tribes that pass through and settle down in Lençóis, the mix of good eating options here is hardly surprising. A great place to sample regional fare is **O Bode** (Praça Horácio de Matos, tel. 75/3334-1600, noon-5pm daily, 7pm-10:30pm daily Dec.-Jan., R$15-25), where you'll find a buffet of local dishes as well as many options featuring the house specialty, *bode* (goat). Among the more exotic local recipes you should try are *godó* (a stew of green bananas and sun-dried beef), *cortado de palma* (diced cactus with ground beef), and a salad of *batata-da-serra,* a local potato found only in the Chapada.

Natora (Praça Horácio de Matos 20, tel. 75/3334-1646, 4pm-1am Sun.-Wed., 10am-1am Fri.-Sat., and daily from Dec.-Mar. and July, R$15-20) serves up a crisp, thin-crust Armenian pizza at outdoor tables that allow you to savor all the action. The freshly made pastas and gnocchis at **Os Artistas da Massa** (Rua da Baderna 49, tel. 75/3334-1886, noon-10pm daily, R$20-30) are as addictive as the cozy ambiance. Note that opening and closing hours (and days) can be irregular. More eclectic is ★ **Cozinha Aberta Slow Food** (Rua da Baderna 111, tel. 75/3334-1066, 12:30pm-11pm daily, R$25-35), where an open kitchen allows diners to watch the preparation of organic local comfort food that draws on Thai, Indian, and Mediterranean cuisines. Service can be as slow as the food. For sweets, head to **Pavé e Comé** (Rua da Baderna 99, tel. 75/3334-1963, 7:30pm-midnight daily). You'll be hard-pressed to choose between the homemade desserts made by Dona Sonia and served inside her lavishly decorated home.

Information and Services

Visit the **Associação dos Condutores de Visitantes de Lençóis** (Rua 10 de Novembro 22, tel. 75/3334-1425, 8am-noon and 2pm-8pm daily) for information and hiring guides. You can also check out the bilingual website www.guialencois.com as well as www.guiachapadadiamantina.com.br (Portuguese only) and www.chapada.org, which offer information about the entire Chapada region along with useful maps. **Guia Turística Chapada Diamantina** (www.guiachapadadiamantina.com.br) is an excellent and very thorough English-language guide filled with maps. Purchase one online or at a tour agency if you plan on spending more than a few days.

Lençóis brims with ecotourism agencies that organize excursions and hire guides. **H20 Adventures** (Rua do Pires, tel. 75/3334-1229, www.h20traveladventures.com) offers a wide variety of excursions; its knowledgeable, English-speaking guides routinely receive raves from adventurous gringos. Aside from trekking, **Nas Alturas** (Praça Horácio de Matos 130, tel. 75/3334-1054, www.nasalturas.net) offers customized expeditions tailored to families, foodies, and birdwatchers. **Fora da Trilha** (Rua das Pedras 202, tel. 75/3334-1326, www.foradatrilha.com) specializes in rock-climbing and rappelling for all levels.

The **Banco do Brasil** at Praça Horácio de Matos is one of the only ATMs in the Chapada Diamantina that accepts foreign cards.

Transportation

You can fly from Salvador to **Aeroporto Coronel Horácio de Matos** (tel. 75/3625-8100), 20 kilometers (12.5 mi) from Lençóis, although flights, with the airline Trip (www.voetrip.com.br, 0800/887-1118), are only offered on Saturday and Sunday mornings. From Salvador's Rodoviária Central, **Real Expresso** (tel. 71/3450-9310, www.realexpresso.com.br, 6.5 hrs, R$60) has four buses at 7am, 1pm, 5pm, and 11pm daily. Extra buses are added during high season. If driving, take BR-324 until Feira de Santana, where you can choose between taking BR-116 until it meets BR-242 or taking BA-052 until Ipirá, following BA-488 until Itaberaba. From this point on, both ways follow BR-242. Whichever route you choose, driving to Lençóis is not for the faint of heart. The roads are often full of potholes and slow-moving trucks.

MUCUGÊ

Smaller and less touristy than Lençóis, Mucugê (named after a native fruit used to make a knockout local liqueur) is another pretty colonial diamond-mining town with its share of nearby natural attractions.

Sights

Aside from pretty 19th-century buildings such as the Prefeitura (city hall) and the Igreja de Santa Isabel, Mucugê possesses the extremely unusual Cimitério Bizantino. Built in 1855 following an outbreak of cholera, the Byzantine style of the snow-white gravestones and monuments of this windswept hillside cemetery is explained by the presence of Turkish diamond traders who lived here. The ensemble is particularly haunting when illuminated at night.

Sports and Recreation

Situated in the heart of the Chapada, Mucugê is at close proximity to numerous natural attractions. Only 5 kilometers (3 mi) away is the Parque Municipal do Mucugê (access via BA-142 toward Andaraí, tel. 75/3338-2156, www.projetosempreviva.com.br, 8am-6pm daily, R$10), a research and cultivation center that doubles as a wildlife reserve. One of the park's main activities is the Projeto Sempre-Viva. The sempre-viva ("forever alive") is a delicate local flower that became a cash cow for locals after the gold rush. Threatened with extinction, commercialization of this delicate blossom was prohibited in 1985; you'll see many growing in the park along with a Museu Vivo do Garimpo, which traces the history of diamond mining in the

region. Within the park, short and easy trails lead to the waterfalls of Piabinhas, Tiburtino, and Andorinhas (the furthest away at one hour), all with natural pools for bathing. Also within 15 kilometers (9 mi) of Mucugê are more waterfalls—Três Barras and Cristais (which together form one of the Chapada's largest swimming holes), Cardoso, Córrego de Pedra (which only flows during the rainy season), Sibéria, and Martinha—all worthy of whiling away a few hours.

Entertainment and Events

Mucugê is reputed for its vibrant Festa de São João (June 23-24) festivities, which include smoky bonfires in the streets, neighbors serving homemade fruit liqueurs from their homes, lots of forró music, and dancing from dusk till dawn. Book accommodations in advance and bundle up, since the longest night of the year can get chilly.

Accommodations and Food

The nicest place to stay in Mucugê is the Pousada Mucugê (Rua Dr. Rodrigues Lima 30, tel. 75/3338-2210, www.pousadamucuge.com.br, R$80-120 d). Well-equipped guest rooms occupy a restored 19th-century mansion in the center of town with a respected restaurant. For delicious regional specialties, try Dona Nena (Rua Direita 140, tel. 75/3338-2143, 11:30am-4pm daily, R$15-25) and Pé de Salsa (Rua Cel. Propércio, tel. 75/3338-2290, 11:30am-2:30pm and 6pm-10:30pm daily, R$8-15).

Information and Services

To book tour guides, visit the Associação dos Condutores de Visitantes de Mucugê (Praça Cel. Propércio, tel. 75/3338-2414, 8am-noon and 2pm-9pm daily), whose building also houses the tourist information center (tel. 75/3338-2255). Km Viagens e Turismo (Praça Cel. Douca Medrado 126, tel. 75/3338-2152, www.kmchapada.com) offers guides as well as taxis and rental cars and motorcycles. Terra Chapada (Rua Dr. Rodrigues Lima, tel. 75/3338-2284, www.terrachapada.com.br)

is a travel agent that can put you in touch with guides and arrange excursions.

Transportation

From Salvador, Águia Branca (tel. 71/4004-1010, www.aguiabranca.com.br) provides direct bus service (8 hours, R$55-71) to Mucugê on weekends; otherwise, you have to change in Itaberaba, where there are two daily departures, in the morning and at night. Driving from Salvador, take BR-324 to Feira de Santana, then BR-242 to the town of Itaberaba, where BA-142 leads to Andaraí and then continues another 50 kilometers (31 mi) to Mucugê.

ANDARAÍ

Between Lençóis and Mucugê, pastel-hued Andaraí is humbler than the other two diamond towns. However, it is surrounded by its share of fantastic natural sights and is the easiest way to get to Igatu, a once-thriving diamond mining town now reduced to a tiny but terribly charming mountain village only 5 kilometers (3 mi) away.

Sights and Recreation

Andaraí is a great point of departure for many of the Chapada Diamantina's star attractions. On the eastern edge of the Sincorá mountain chain, it is perfectly situated for those who want to go trekking through the Vale do Paty. It is also less than 10 kilometers (6 mi) from Marimbus, a swamp-like ecosystem created by the Rio Santo Antônio. The best way to get around the area is by hiring a guide with a canoe (2.5 hours, R$20), then gliding through the waters adorned with oversized Victoria amazonica lily pads and giant water ferns. A few kilometers outside of town is the Cachoeira de Ramalho, a medium-to-difficult trek along an ancient miners' trail surrounded by natural pools. Farther afield (20 km/12.5 mi) is the Cachoeira do Roncador, featuring pools sculpted out of rose quartz, reached after an easy hike.

Those with a penchant for the color blue

should visit Poço Encantado. (8pm-4pm daily, R$20), 40 kilometers (25 mi) from Andaraí on the road to Itaeté. When illuminated by sunlight (10am-1:30pm daily Apr.-Sept.), the intense cobalt hue of its waters is truly "enchanting." The added advantage of Poço Azul (8pm-5pm daily, R$15)—whose waters also turn dazzling blue when hit by the sun's rays (12:30pm-2:30pm daily Feb.-Oct.)—is that you can swim or snorkel (R$15). Before you take the plunge, make sure to reserve a delicious home-cooked meal prepared by Dona Alice (tel. 75/8163-8292), whose home lies at the entrance to the property. Poço Azul is around 50 kilometers (31 mi) from Andaraí on the road to Itaeté.

Accommodations and Food

The Pousada Sincorá (Av. Paraguassu 120, tel. 75/3335-2210, www.sincora.com.br, R$115 d) is a warm and appealingly decorated old house that is rightly proud of its hearty "colonial" breakfasts. The owners also have a farm in the Marimbus wetland where guests can camp or go on guided canoe tours. For light food and delicious homemade ice cream featuring rare flavors such as jenipapo, cachaça, and rapadura (caramelized sugar cane), visit the Sorveteria Apollo (Praça Raul Dantas 1, tel. 75/3335-2256, 9am-8pm).

Transportation and Services

For guides and tourist information, contact the Associação dos Condutores de Visitantes de Andaraí (Rua Dr. José Gonçalves Cincorá, tel. 75/3335-2225, 8am-noon and 2pm-5pm daily).

Andaraí is about 100 kilometers (62 mi) from Lençóis (to the north, via BR-242 and BA-142) and around 50 kilometers (31 mi) from Mucugê (to the south along BR-142). From Salvador, Águia Branca (tel. 71/4004-1010, www.aguiabranca.com.br) provides direct bus service (7 hours, R$66) to Andaraí on weekends; otherwise, you'll need to change in Itaberaba. Driving from Salvador, take BR-324 to Feira de Santana, then BR-242 to the town of Itaberaba, where BA-142 leads to Andaraí.

IGATU

During the height of its 19th-century diamond rush, thriving Igatu had a population of 3,000. Today it's a small village of 350 where *Flintstones*-like stone houses alternate with pretty pastel villas, all of which are surrounded by the lush fruit and vegetable gardens that supply much of the local produce. As for the splendor of its past, it has been reduced to a bewitchingly haunted area of ruined stone mansions overgrown with mango trees and wild orchids.

Sights

Amid Igatu's ruins, the Galeria Arte & Memória (Rua Luís dos Santos, tel. 75/3335-2510, 9am-6pm daily, R$2) exhibits found objects and equipment used by the diamond miners as well as contemporary artwork by regional artists inside a beautiful space built on the ruins of a stone house. A garden shelters local flora, contemporary sculptures, and an enticing café where you can linger over crepes and cappuccino. For more insight into the town's diamond legacy, tour the nearby Mina Brejo-Verruga (7am-5pm daily, R$5), the biggest mine in the region, where—helmeted and armed with a flashlight—you can snake your way through a hand-dug tunnel stretching 400 meters (1,300 feet) into the side of a mountain. In the main chamber, 20 clay markers, each with a candle, pays homage to the miners who died here. The return to daylight will be a shock, which you can alleviate with a swim in the Poço do Brejo. Back in town, visit Ponto do Amarildo (Rua Sete de Setembro, tel. 75/3335-7017, noon-2pm and 5pm-10pm Mon.-Fri., 8am-10pm Sat.-Sun.), an eccentric emporium that local character Amarildo dos Santos has created in the living room of his house. The shelves are crammed with everything from homemade *doces* and *licores* to odd bits of local memorabilia and Amarildo's own hand-painted books recounting tales of Igatu.

Accommodations and Food

The best *pousada* here is the lovely and very comfortable Pousada Pedras de Igatu (Rua São Sebastião, tel. 75/3335-2281, R$120-170), which has a swimming pool and a sauna (but no TV) and terrific views of the surrounding countryside. Cheaper but charming is Hospedagem Flor de Açucena (Rua Nova, tel. 75/3335-7003, R$80-120), located in a rustic stone house whose guest rooms overlook a garden and pool. A kitchen and bathrooms are available for those who want to camp in the garden. Also ask around for rooms to rent with locals; many will cook local specialties for you on their wood stoves using produce grown in their gardens. A great option for home-cooked fare is Água Boa (Rua Nova 13, tel. 75/3335-7013, 10am-10pm daily, R$15-25), a family-run spot where you can dig into *godó* (finely diced and cooked green banana flavored with sun-dried beef) and *galinha caipira* (a rich chicken stew).

Transportation

Igatu can only be reached by a rocky trail that turns off BA-142 from Mucugê or from Andaraí. In either case, you'll need a 4WD vehicle or the stamina required for a couple of hours of uphill hiking. However, when you arrive at this remote town suspended in the mountains, you'll be more than compensated for the hardships of the journey.

CAPÃO (CAETÉ-AÇU)

Hugging the northwest edge of the Parque Nacional da Chapada Diamantina, Caeté-Açu (commonly referred to as Capão, after the valley in which it sits) is a tranquil village that in recent years has attracted a mellow expat community of New Agers, artists, hippies, and gringos who live in harmony with the spectacular surroundings. Aside from its bucolic air, it's a starting point for treks to some of the park's most impressive natural attractions, including the Cachoeira da Fumaça.

Sights and Recreation

One of the indisputable highlights of the Chapada, the Cachoeira da Fumaça is a waterfall so high that most of its water evaporates to mist before hitting the ground (hence its name, "Smoke Waterfall"). Looking down on the cascading water from above involves a long but scenic 6-kilometer (3.7-mi) hike from Capão. Getting right beneath it is even more arduous, involving a three-day trek (with a guide, supplies, and camping gear) through the breathtakingly beautiful Vale do Capão.

An easier outing is to Poço Angélica, a natural pool surrounded by lush vegetation that's only a 15-minute walk from Vila do Bomba, a village 8 kilometers (5 mi) from Capão (whose narrow road can be difficult to navigate). Closer to town is the Cachoeira do Rio Preto, a small cascade with a pool, located 4 kilometers (1.5 mi) from the center of town.

Accommodations and Food

There are a handful of pleasantly rustic places to stay in Capão. Pousada Vila Esperança (Rua dos Gatos, tel. 75/3344-1384, www.vilaesperanca.com.br, R$100-150 d) is an appealing choice set amid an orchard of fruit trees with a small creek in back. Tatami mats and the presence of *yakkissoba* on the menu betray the owner's Japanese origins. Close to the main square, Pousada Pé No Mato (tel. 75/3344-1105, www.penomato.com.br, R$100-140 d, R$40-50 pp) is a friendly combo hostel/ecotour agency with accommodations for two, three, and four people in individual chalets, sustainably fashioned out of adobe and reforested native woods and surrounded by native vegetation. It's popular with foreign backpackers for its organic breakfasts made with garden produce. The most luxurious option is Pousada Vila Lagoa das Cores (Rua da Lagoa, tel. 75/3344-1114, www.lagoadascores.com.br, R$280-480 d), located 2.5 kilometers (1.6 mi) outside of town in an idyllic natural

setting with views of Morro Branco mountain. Charmingly decorated bungalows, soap made with aromatic herbs grown on the premises, a holistic spa, and organic produce at the superb restaurant all complement the personalized service.

Capão's famed culinary specialty is the *pastel de palmito de jaca,* a pastry stuffed with "green" (i.e., unripe) jackfruit cooked and seasoned with herbs. You'll find it all over town, but the woman who invented it is Dona Dalva (Praça São Sebastião, tel. 75/3344-1140, 9am-9pm daily). Also famous is the healthy (and gigantic!) whole-wheat crust pizza served at Pizza Integral do Capão (Praça São Sebastião, tel. 75/3344-1138, 4pm-11pm daily, R$15-20). For a tasty home-cooked meal, head to the welcoming house of Dona Beli (Rua do Folga 140, tel. 75/3344-1085, noon-8pm daily, R$15-20), where dishes of the day are accompanied by local exotica such as sautéed *palma* (cactus) and *jaca;* expect lines on holidays.

Transportation and Services

To book tour guides, visit the Associação dos Condutores de Visitantes do Vale do Capão (Rua Campos, 75/3344-1087) or contact Tatu na Trilha (Rua da Vila, tel. 75/3344-1124), which also organizes trekking expeditions. There are no banks with ATMs in Capão; for cash withdrawals you'll need to go to Palmeiras.

From Salvador, Real Expresso (tel. 71/3450-9310, www.realexpresso.com.br) provides four daily departures to Palmeiras (7 hours, R$67). Buses also leave from Lençóis (1 hour, R$6). From Palmeiras, local vans for Capão cost R$10 pp. Driving from Salvador, take BR-324 to Feira de Santana, then BR-242 to Palmeiras (passing Itaberaba and Lençóis), from which a 21-kilometer (12-mi) dirt road leads to Capão.

The coast leading south from Salvador down to Bahia's border with Espírito Santo is the longest—and perhaps most beautiful—coastline in Brazil. Beaches, beaches, and more beaches are the big draw. From the party scenes of Porto Seguro and Morro de São Paulo, passing through the drowsy colonial charms of Ilhéus and Caravelas, to the sensation of being lost in paradise provoked by the likes of Boipeba and Caraíva, reserve a week (or two), stock up on SPF 60, and start exploring.

MORRO DE SÃO PAULO

For more than 20 years, this once-tiny fishing village on the Ilha de Tinhare has been the most popular destination along the Dendê Coast—named after the *dendê* palm, whose fruit produces the amber-colored oil used in traditional Bahian cooking—that stretches from Valença south to Itacaré. During the summer, it is mobbed by sand- and sun-worshippers from all over, and "Morro" (as it is called) becomes party central. If this isn't your scene, don't completely give up on Morro de São Paulo. In the off-season, especially during the week, it's possible to surrender to the simpler pleasures offered by swaths of native Atlantic forest, coral reefs, and warm ocean pools. And there are no cars, a big plus (you can hire a wheelbarrow to lug your baggage for R$10 per piece).

Beaches

Most visitors arrive by boat in Morro and are greeted by the grandiose stone gates of an early 17th-century ruined fortress and a 19th-century lighthouse, from whose lofty heights sunset gazing (and applauding) has become a ritual. The rest of the village is urbanized, densely packed with restaurants, *pousadas,* and stores. Follow the main drag of Rua Caminho da Praia to arrive at the beginning of a quintet of nameless but distinctive numbered beaches. Primeira Praia (First Beach) is the closest to the village and is where most of the local families hang out. Segunda Praia (Second Beach) is lined with restaurants, clubs, and beach bars that throb with raves and luaus all night. By day it's full of hip young things knocking around soccer balls, volleyballs, and frescoballs. Terceira Praia (Third Beach) is somewhat more tranquil and has some of the best water for diving. Boat excursions depart from here. Half an hour from the village, Quarta Praia (Fourth Beach) offers 4 kilometers (2.5 mi) of coconut-fringed sand, which starts out developed and peters out into delicious seclusion. The best-preserved (and most gorgeous) of them all, Quinta Praia (Fifth Beach), also known as Praia do Encanto, involves a long two-hour trek that can only be undertaken at low tide (or by mule-drawn carts from Terceira Praia, R$30 for 2 people). Aside from a small handful of upscale *pousadas,* its sands are deserted.

Sports and Recreation

The best way to take advantage of Morro's natural attractions is by boat. The most popular trip is a full-day outing (R$80) around Tinhare island: stops include the offshore reefs of Garapuá and Moreré, the beaches of Cueira, Tassimirim, and Boca da Barra (all on the island of Boipeba), and then the pretty town of Cairu with its 17th-century Convento de Santo Antônio (the second oldest convent in Brazil). Throughout the day, there are ample opportunities for swimming, snorkeling, and feasting on fresh oysters from floating oyster bars anchored in the Rio do Inferno. Another highlight is diving amidst the reefs in the clear, shallow waters off Primeira and Terceira Praias, which you can do by day or night for R$75-130 pp with an instructor. For more information about excursions or diving, contact Itha do Mar (Rua da Prainha 11, tel. 75/3652-1104).

An easy 40-minute hike (during low tide) from Morro leads to the tranquil fishing village of Gamboa, from where you can easily reach the Fonte do Céu waterfall. The trail passes by cliffs of colored clay, where you can give yourself a purifying facial—or "claycial." You can rent a boat to sail in the bay at Clube de Vela de Gamboa (tel. 75/3653-7131, R$45-95/hour), with or without an instructor.

Accommodations

There's no shortage of accommodations on Morro de São Paulo. Rates listed are for the off-season, but high-season prices are much steeper. Although Morro is famed for its beaches, it's worth trading beachfront access for one of the trio of simple yet fetching private guest rooms at Villa-Bahia Apartments (Rua Porto de Cima, tel. 75/8169-6532, www.vila-bahia.com, R$120-180 d), an expertly run B&B perched on a hilltop above Morro's main square. German owner Werner plays tropical host to the hilt, dishing up advice as well as lavish homemade breakfasts on a balcony with spectacular views. Boasting the same spectacular views is neighboring Pousada Aquarela (Rua Porto de Cima, tel. 75/3652-1509, www.pousadadoaquarela.com, R$110-150 d), whose bright and breezy guest rooms boast hammock-strung verandas and sleep up to four. An enticing on-site restaurant overlooking the jungle is a bonus. To be right in the middle of the action on Segunda Praia (but still get some shut eye), try Pousada Villa dos Graffitis (tel. 75/3652-1803, www.villadosgraffitis.com.br, R$240-360 d). At this funky newcomer, graffiti adorns the sleekly minimalist rooms (which sleep up to five). Its off-beach location ensures sleep, while the pool, lounge, and fresh breakfasts are ideal hangover cures. On Terceira Praia, Hotel Fazenda Vila Guaiamu (tel. 75/3652-1035, www.vilaguaiamu.com.br, July-Apr., R$180-230 d) feels miles from the nearby mayhem. A sprinkling of whitewashed chalets scattered amid the rustling palms of a former coconut plantation are home to clean, if somewhat worn guest rooms as well as namesake

guiamus, blue-hued crabs who emerge from their holes to feed at the beginning and end of the day. The on-site restaurant does a mean *moqueca.*

For a resort experience, head to the Pousada Villa dos Corais (tel. 75/3652-1560, www.villadoscorais.com.br, R$430-490 d) with an enviable location straddling both Terceira and Quarta Praias. The 40 bungalows are spacious, airy, and comfortable, with king beds, noiseless air-conditioning, and verandas with hammocks. Two restaurants, a pool bar and beach bar, tennis courts, a games room, library, sauna, and steam room round out the amenities. Located on utterly dreamy Quinta Praia, the nine fully equipped eco-chalets at ★ Anima Hotel (tel. 75/3652-2077, www.animahotel.com, July-May, R$340-410 d) are the epitome of back-to-nature chic, though you might feel a little isolated. The hotel offers snorkel masks and binoculars so you can commune with the exotic fish and birds sharing your ecosystem.

Food

During the day, food options are mostly geared toward classic Bahian beach fare, such as the fried fish, crab, shrimp, and *moquecas* served at many *barracas*. For some of the best fish and seafood dishes around, try Club do Balanço (10am-7pm daily Mar.-June and Aug.-Dec., 10am-midnight daily Jan.-Feb. and July) on trendy Segunda Praia. Fans of Quarta Praia swear by Bar das Piscinas (9am-6pm daily) and Pimenta Rosa (10am-5pm daily).

At night, culinary pleasures are taken more seriously. For both lunch and dinner, Sabor da Terra (Rua Caminho da Praia, tel. 75/3652-1156, noon-midnight daily, R$20-30), on the town's main drag, beckons with its wide veranda, perfect for people-watching, and the fragrance of well-seasoned Bahian fish and seafood dishes such as *moqueca* and *bobó de camarão.* The wafting scent of freshly baked pizza emerging from a wood oven will lure you to Restaurante e Pizzeria Bianco e Nero (Rua Caminho da Praia, tel. 75/3652-1097, lunch Tues.-Sun., dinner daily, R$20-30).

For the perfect finishing touch, stop by Dona Bárbara's sweet stand (in front of Sabor da Terra) and stock up on homemade goodies such as *brigadeiro, cocadas,* and *quejadinhas.*

Information

There is a tourist office at Praça Aureliano Lima (tel. 75/3652-1083, www.morrosp.com. br, 8am-10pm daily). You can also check out www.morrodesaopaulobrasil.com.br. Although there are a few ATMs, they can run out of money during holidays; while it's a good idea to have some spare cash, many places accept credit cards.

Transportation

Both high-speed catamarans and *lanchas rápidas* offer daily transportation from Salvador's Terminal Marítimo in front of the Mercado Modelo. The trip (2.5 hrs, R$80) is scenic, but the ocean can be quite choppy. In Salvador, contact Catamarã Biotur (tel. 75/3641-3327, www.biotur.com.br), Catamarã Farol da Barra (tel. 71/3319-4570, www.faroldomorrotour.com), Lancha Lula Lu (tel. 75/9917-1975), Lancha Ilha Bela (tel. 71/3326-7158, www.ilhabelatm.com.br), or the Terminal Marítimo (tel. 71/3319-2890). From Salvador, you can take a small eight-seater plane (20 min., R$320 pp) operated by Addey Taxi Aéreo (tel. 71/3204-1393, www.addey.tur. br). You must pay a visitor's tax (R$15) upon arrival on the island.

Águia Branca (tel. 71/4004-1010, www. aguiabranca.com.br) and Viação Cidade Sul (tel. 71/3682-1791, www.viacaocidadesol. com.br) both provide hourly bus service from Bom Despacho (the bus station located at the ferry terminal on the island of Itaparica) to the nearby town of Valença (2 hours, around R$18). From Valença's docks, numerous boats (1.5 hours, R$7) and *lanchas* (30 min., R$16) make the trip to Morro daily 7am-6pm.

ILHA DE BOIPEBA

Although only the Rio do Inferno (River of Hell) separates Ilha de Boipeba from the Ilha do Tinhare, where Morro de São Paulo is located, Boipeba is Morro as it was 20 years ago before an influx of tourism blew everything out of proportion. Its beautiful unspoiled beaches are framed by lush jungle and crisscrossed by warm rivers that are ideal for bathing. Although Boipeba is becoming a hip beach resort for those in the know, it has managed to retain a bucolic tranquility along with some 20 kilometers (12 mi) of secluded white-sand beaches protected by coral reefs.

Sights and Recreation

The most "developed" of Boipeba's beaches—which, thankfully, isn't saying much—is Boca da Barra. Here, where the Rio do Inferno meets the sea, you'll find lots of *barracas* where you can dig into fresh fish and seafood while soaking in fresh water. Heading south, a half-hour walk brings you to the sugary white sands of Tassimirim, followed by the blissfully deserted Praia de Cueira, the island's best swimming beach. Another 1.5 hours' walk (easier undertaken during low tide) brings you to idyllic Morerê, where the shade of a giant almond tree offers respite from the sun, and an hour more brings you to Bainema, a deserted beach fringed by coconut palms and lush vegetation. Another 30 minutes away is Ponta dos Castelhanos, a great diving destination with coral reefs and a 16th-century Spanish shipwreck to explore. Apart from walking, it's possible to take boat trips to all of these beaches from the docks at Boca da Barra. A trip to Ponta de Castelhanos costs around R$40, while a journey around the entire island will set you back R$60. You can also sail up the Rio do Sapé and around the surrounding mangroves in a dug-out canoe (R$30 for 2 hours). It's possible to journey overland via bumpy tractor-trucks between Velha Boipeba and Moreré; depending on the number of passengers, expect to pay R$5-10.

Accommodations and Food

The languorous village of Velha Boipeba, whose epicenter is the 17th-century Igreja do Divino Espírito Santo, offers both simple and more sophisticated accommodations for visitors, as does Moreré, a tiny fishing village that's a 90-minute walk or 40-minute boat or tractor ride away.

Owned by two American brothers from Queens, Pousada Santa Clara (tel. 75/3653-6085, www.santaclaraboipeba.com, R$140-170 d, closed June) offers a dozen cozily minimalist guest rooms set amidst a lush tropical garden. Brother Mark is the culinary genius behind the romantic Restaurante Santa Clara; he plans internationally inspired daily dinner options based on the fresh catch available (lobster, shrimp, fish). Practically next door, Pousada Vila Sereia (tel. 75/3653-6045, www.vilasereia.com.br, R$280-350) is more intimate but equally well run by Chris, a São Paulo transplant. A quartet of private, ingeniously outfitted, and candy-colored palm-thatched bungalows (sleep up to four) are situated right on Boca da Barra beach. Wake in the morning to a tropical breakfast banquet arrayed upon your private veranda.

At ★ Eco-Pousada Casa Bobô (tel. 75/9930-5757, www.pousadacasabobo.com, R$180-280 d), Catalan/Brazilian owners Myriam and Nilton preside over a trio of sustainably built, eco-chic bungalows nestled atop the jungly slopes of Monte Alegre with views of the jade waters of Moreré beach, 15 minutes away. For those who can't get enough of Nilton's organic cuisine, half-board accommodation is available. Right on Moreré beach, Restaurante Mar e Coco (tel. 75/3653-6094, 10am-6pm daily, R$25-35) offers an idyllic setting in which to take shelter from the midday sun in the crustacean company of succulent shrimp and plantain *moquecas* and seafood stroganoffs. In the same vein, but more primitive, is the Barraca do Guido (tel. 75/9907-7049, 8am-5pm daily, R$20-30), located on Praia da Cueira, where the specialty is freshly caught lobster cooked over an open flame and served with butter or pineapple. Back in town, don't leave Boipeba without trying the island's most famous *sorvete,* made out of local *mangaba* fruit at Picolé do Pinto (Rua do Areal, tel. 75/3653-6119, noon-10pm daily), in the village of Velha Boipeba.

Information

Many hotels can organize guides or trips, including activities such as canoeing, horseback riding, taking nature walks through the Atlantic forest, or snorkeling in the tidal pools. For boating trips, talk to local fishermen down at the docks. For more information, consult the multilingual website www.

Ilha de Boipeba

ilhadeboipeba.org.br and www.boipeba.tur. br. There are no banks on the island, so stock up on cash.

Transportation

Difficult access to Boipeba has helped keep the tourist crush at bay. From Valença's docks you can take a boat (4 hours, R$14), with one daily departure at noon, or smaller, motorized *lanchas* (30 minutes, R$38), with more frequent daily departure (especially during high season). Another option is to take a bus to the town of Torrinhas and then board a ferry (1.5 hours, R$15) or *lancha* (20 minutes, R$80) for Boipeba, which stops in the colonial town of Cairu. From Morro de São Paulo, tour operators offer daily boat trips that stop at Boipeba; you can organize it so that you can stay for more than a day. Another alternative is to take a one-hour Jeep ride and then a quick boat across the river to Boipeba, a service offered by Bahia Terra (Segunda Praia, 75/3653-6017, www.boipebatur.com.br, R$95 pp). Quicker, more comfortable, and more expensive is to fly directly from Salvador to Boipeba in a small plane operated by Addey Taxi Aéreo (tel. 71/3204-1393, www.addey. tur.br, 30 minutes, R$370 pp).

PENÍNSULA DE MARAÚ

Squeezed between the Bay of Camamu and the open Atlantic, the Maraú peninsula is a region of great natural beauty composed of islands, lagoons, dunes, and mangrove swamps. The easiest way to explore the area is by traveling to the mainland city of Camamu, 330 kilometers (205 mi) south of Salvador, and then taking a boat across the Bay of Camamu to the fishing village and main resort town of Barra Grande.

★ Barra Grande

Despite the increase of *pousadas,* restaurants, and trendy young vacationers from southern Brazil who flock here in the summer for some hippie-flavored R&R, this relaxing fishing village, with its main drag of soft sand leading down to fluffy beaches, is still deliciously unspoiled. Barra Grande is a great place to unwind as well as explore Brazil's third largest bay (after Salvador's Baía de Todos os Santos and Rio's Guanabara). From the town, you can wander endlessly along the coast.

Sights and Recreation

Praia do Barra Grande all but disappears during high tide; other, more secluded beaches are reachable by foot. Walk toward the open Atlantic to reach Ponta do Mutá, which marks the northern tip of the peninsula before veering south and passing reef-lined Três Coqueiros and idyllic Bombaça with both rough waves and protected natural pools. A 2.5-hour walk from Barra, Taipu de Fora routinely racks up accolades as one of Brazil's most stunning beaches due to a combination of shimmering turquoise waters and coral-lined pools flooded with brightly hued fish (rent snorkel equipment from beach vendors). Taipu is often packed with tourists; if you continue another 6 kilometers (3.5 mi), you'll find a remote refuge amidst the more secluded sands of Cassange. Open trucks known as *jardineiras* shuttle passengers between Barra Grande and Taipu (R$10 pp).

Apart from beachcombing, you can explore the Baía de Camamu's more far-flung attractions by land or by sea. In the absence of paved roads, the former involves walking or catching a ride with a dune buggy or *jardineiras,* which leave from Rua Vasco Neto. Road-trip excursions stop at Taipu de Fora as well as Morro Bela Vista, a lush hilltop with panoramic views and terrific sunset watching; and Lagoa de Cassange, a freshwater lake in the midst of Sahara-like dunes. An equally unforgettable experience is taking a full-day boat trip around the bay with stops at many islands. Excursions usually leave early in the morning and cost R$30 for a boat and R$60 for a high-speed *lancha.* For information, contact Camamu Adventure (Av. Beira Mar, tel. 73/3258-6236, www.camamuadventure.com.br).

Accommodations

For a great location with access to the beach

and the village, try simple and friendly Pousada Tubarão (Rua Vasco Neto 92, tel. 73/3258-6006, pousadatutti.com.br, R$140-220 d), whose casual restaurant also serves delicious fare in the tropical garden or on the beach. Owned by a friendly young Italian couple, Denada Posada (Rua Vasco Neto 10, tel. 73/3258-6444, www.denadaposada.com, R$250-350 d) features eight clean and stylish bungalows decked out in wood and natural fibers; a small pool and restaurant serve up views and Italian food. Flat Bahia (Rua José Melo Pirajá, tel. 73/3258-6124, www.flatbarra.com.br, R$115-140 d) offers 10 cheery and spacious apartments with verandas, living rooms, and equipped kitchens—rustle up your own freshly caught fish 24/7, but still have your sheets changed. Common areas include a lounge, pool, barbecue area, and garden, where breakfast is served.

Taipu de Fora's stunning beach lures its own share of (somewhat upscale) eco-accommodations. Among the nicest is appropriately named Dreamland Bungalows (tel. 73/3258-6087, www.dreamland-brasil.com, R$320-360 d), with breezy, modern two-story villas within spitting distance of the sand. Even closer is the beach bar/restaurant decked out with rustic lounge furniture where friendly Norwegian owner/lapsed rock 'n roller Yan takes time out from hosting duties to flaunt his guitar skills. Those seeking serious yet sustainable seclusion will fall hard for the ★ Butterfly House (tel. 73/3258-6087, www.dreamland-brasil.com, R$420-800 d). Located on a lush estate just off unspoiled Cassange beach, this eco-boutique *pousada* is the brainchild of Chloe Gibbs, a former British nurse and fervent ecologist who spent close to a decade turning her dream into reality (she even fashioned the bathroom sinks herself at a local ceramics factory!). The results wed environmentalism (grass thatched roofs, solar-heated water, recycled everything) with an exquisite decorative sensibility that deftly fuses French, Moroccan, Indian, and local elements throughout the pool area, bar, gazebo, and

Anna Banana, an organic fusion restaurant serving delicious meals.

Food

Near the main square, A Tapera (Rua Dra Lili, tel. 75/3258-6119, www.atapera.com.br, 1pm-11pm daily Dec.-Feb., 1pm-10pm Wed.-Mon. Mar.-Nov., closed May, R$25-40) is a favorite for fish and a delicious squid and octopus *moqueca*. At her pretty namesake outdoor restaurant, Donanna (Rua do Anjo, tel. 75/3258-6407, noon-10pm Mon.-Sat., noon-midnight daily Dec.-Feb., closed June, R$25-35), owner-chef Dona Ana concocts unusual seafood delicacies such as ginger-mango fish and shrimp in coconut sauce. Scrumptious pizza and other freshly made Italian dishes are served at Pinocchio (Praça do Tamarindo, tel. 73/3258-6248, dinner daily, R$20-30), whose outdoor candlelit tables are spread beneath an enormous tamarind tree. At secluded Bombaça beach, just before the more touristy Taipus de Fora, the Tocossauro Bar (tel. 73/3528-6047, 9am-6:30pm daily) is an enticing "surf" bar-restaurant belonging to the Pousada Kaluana, where you can chill out beneath whispering palms.

Information

Head to the Secretaria de Turismo de Maraú (Av. José Melo Pirajá, tel. 73/3258-2131) for info about Barra Grande and the surrounding peninsula. For information in English, www.barra-grande.net is a great website with lots of listings and maps. Bring lots of cash since there are no banks or ATMs (the closest are in Camamu).

Transportation

The easiest, but longest, way to get to Barra Grande is to take a ferry from Salvador's Terminal Marítimo to Bom Despacho on the Ilha da Itaparica. At the docks, there is a bus station where companies such as Águia Branca (tel. 71/4004-1010, www.aguiabranca.com.br) and Viação Cidade Sol (tel. 71/3682-1791, www.viacaocidadesol.com.br) have buses departing almost hourly between 5am-6pm to Camamu (3.5 hours, R$31). At Camamu's dock, during the day frequent slow boats (1.5 hours, R$6) and fast *lanchas* (40 minutes, R$30) make the scenic trip across the Rio Acarai to Barra Grande. It is also possible to reach Barra Grande by land, going north along a dirt road from Itacaré. This requires chartering a Jeep or other 4WD vehicle, which is expensive (around R$100 pp) and slow-going.

ITACARÉ

Until 1998, when a paved highway opened up access to Itacaré from Ilhéus, 70 kilometers (43 mi) to the south, Itacaré was a remote fishing village straddling the mouth of the Rio de Contas. Its stunning beaches backed by native Atlantic forest were a well-guarded secret known to only a few hard-core surfers and getaway artists. Since then, the secret has gotten out, and Itacaré has become one of the biggest "it" beaches on the Bahian coast.

Beaches

Itacaré's 15 pristine beaches are set off by dramatic hillsides carpeted in lush green vegetation. Many—such as the urban beaches of Resende, Tiririca, Praia do Costa and Praia do Ribeira—are only a few hundred meters' walk from Itacaré's center. Those closest to town—especially the nerve center that is Praia da Concha—can get pretty crowded in the summer, littered as they are with *pousadas* and bars playing trance-inducing electronic music. However, the farther you get, the more deserted the beaches become. Hiking through virgin forest to the best of these *praias de fora* (outer beaches)—such as the idyllic Prainha, reached by a 45-minute jungle trail that begins at Praia do Ribeira—is part of the unique Itacaré experience.

The bustling main drag of Rua Pedro Longo and its continuation (known as the Caminho das Praias) links the urban beaches. You can reach more far-flung beaches on foot or by the municipal bus (R$2.50) that leaves Centro hourly and runs along highway BA-001 in the direction of Ilhéus. Some trails to

the beaches pass through private property, and you'll be charged a small access fee. Due to poor signage and isolation (and security issues), it's best to go in the company of a guide or a local. Many tour agencies run "best of" beach day trips for around R$50 pp.

Itacaré has some of the finest waves in the Brazilian Northeast. Surfers will go gaga over Prainha (3 km/2 mi) and its neighbors, Praia São José (6 km/3.5 mi) and Praia Jeribucaçu (7 km/4 mi), as well as the particularly beautiful Praia Havaizinho and Praia de Engenhoca, roughly 12 kilometers (7.5 mi) from town. If you don't want complete seclusion, Itacarezinho, 15 kilometers (9 mi) away and accessible by bus, has a sprinkling of beach *barracas* where you can kick back with a caipirinha and refresh yourself in the sparkling freshwater pool formed by the Tijuípe waterfall. Easy Drop (Rua João Coutinho 140, tel. 73/3251-3065, www.easydrop.com) is a surf school where a four-day package, including transportation and equipment, costs R$225 per day. To rent your own gear, contact Thor Surf Point (Rua Pedro Longo 574, tel. 73/3251-2057).

Sports and Recreation

Tree-trekking aficionados will enjoy channeling Tarzan at the activities circuit located in the middle of Praia da Ribeira's Atlantic rain forest. Conduru Ecoturismo (Praça da Bandeira 89, tel.73/3251-3089, www.conduruecoturimso.com.br) offers various radical sports activities on Praia do Ribeira, including ziplining over the beach (four rides, R$40). Rappelling at the Noré waterfall (R$40) is another popular adrenaline-charged outing, as is rafting down the Rio de Contas; Ativa Rafting (Rua Pé da Pancada, tel. 73/3257-2083, www.ativarafting.com.br) charges R$75 for a full-day outing. Those seeking more mellow vibes can rent a canoe and paddle through the coastal mangrove swamps to the Cachoeira do Engenho waterfall (6 hours, R$55). EcoTrip (Rua João Coutinho 235, tel. 73/3251-2191, www.ecotrip.tur.br) offers many of these outings throughout the region.

Accommodations

Since the paved highway to Ilhéus opened, Itacaré has been flooded with *pousadas*, from backpackers' refuges to tropically chic eco-resorts. Prices listed are for off-season. Some of the most inexpensive options—and also those closest to the action—are along the Rua Pedro Longo. More upscale options are sheltered within the confines of the leafy Condomínio Conchas do Mar complex.

The Casarão Verde Hostel's (Av. Praça Castro Alves 7, tel. 73/3251-2037, www. casaraoverdehostel.com R$60-70 d, R$26-38 pp) renovated dorms and private rooms occupy a turn-of-the-20th-century mansion overlooking the harbor. Aside from cathedral-high ceilings, polished wood floors, and stained glass windows, guests can take advantage of a kitchen, barbecue area, mini-gym, and elegant gardens. At Pousada Casa Tiki (Rua C 30, Conchas do Mar, tel. 73/9810-6098, www.pousadadacasatiki.com.br, R$100-150 d), outgoing young expats, Kevin and Pati, instill a casual vibe and a Polynesian tiki bar aesthetic at their tropical B&B. Guests are invited to sit around a big log table swapping stories over fresh fruit juice and petting the *pousada* pooches. More boutiquey than tiki is the lovely Pousada Burundanga (Qd. D. Lot. 6, Conchas do Mar, tel. 73/3251-2543, www.burundanga.com.br, R$215-275 d). Spacious bungalows are tastefully decorated with local *artesanato* and furnishings hewed out of local wood. From the hammock on your private deck, gaze onto a tangle of jungle visited by birds and monkeys

Pousada Tânara (tel. 73/3251-3423, www.pousadatanara.com, R$150-290 d), around 2 kilometers (1.2 mi) from town, is a favorite with the international and surfing crowd. In indigenous Pataxó, Tânara means "nature," evidenced by six rustic rooms that sit immersed in greenery, tumbling onto the surfer's paradise of Praia de Tiririca. Lodgings are attractive, but some are quite tight. It's a quick walk to town by day, but a taxi is recommended at night. ★ Art Jungle Eco Lodge (Rod. Ilhéus-Itacaré km 63, tel.

73/9905-7775, artjungle.com.br, R$120-220 d) consists of a handful of magical storybook-come-to-life tropical bungalows (including a couple of bonafide tree houses!) near the shores of Rio de Contas, yet only a five-minute drive from Itacaré. Transportation can be organized, while renting a car keeps you from feeling cut off from civilization— but if that's your mission, you'll be in heaven. There are no phones, TV, air-conditioning, or Internet, just hummingbirds, silence, sea views, and a pool and sauna.

Live it up and wind down at the same time at the happily un-resorty Txai Resort (tel. 73/2101-5000, www.txai.com.br, R$1,100-2,200 d). Located 16 kilometers (10 mi) from Itacaré, the rambling palmy grounds of this former cocoa plantation gaze onto the unspoiled white sands of Itacarezinho beach. Its 40 spacious, simple bungalows and creatively decorated main lounges merge traditional architecture and organic materials with understated luxury. There is a pool as well as yoga and alternative healing therapies at a stunning hilltop spa. While service is attentive, food is hit-and-miss.

Food

Take a seat (and be prepared to wait) at Estrela d'Alva (Rua Pedro Longo 568, tel. 73/9909-1191, lunch and dinner daily, R$15-25) and Flor do Cacau (Rua Pedro Longo 4800, tel. 73/9945-4800, lunch and dinner daily, R$15-25) for tasty, authentic Bahian fare such as *bobó* and *moqueca de camarão*, served in robust portions with *farofa, banana da terra*, and *feijão*. The hot and cold buffet offerings at Casa de Taipa (Rua Pedro Longo 345, tel. 73/3251-3510, noon-10pm daily, R$22) are more diverse, and you can refill your plate as many times as you want. For Arab, vegetarian fare, try Alamaim (Rua Pedro Longo 203, 73/3251-3462, www.restaurantealamaim.com. br, 2:30pm-10pm Mon.-Sat., R$15-25).

Come sundown, a popular stop for the young and famished is Tio Gu Caféça (Rua Pedro Longo 488, 73/3251-2084, www.tiogu. com, 5pm-midnight Wed.-Mon., R$15-25), specializing in fresh fruit juices, salads, and generously stuffed, sweet and savory crepes named after the region's beaches. At the fare end of the harbor is a colonial blue mansion home to Café e Boteco da Vila (Rua Castro Alves 35, tel. 73/9915-3574, 6pm-midnight Sun.-Thurs., 5pm-2am Fri.-Sat., R$15-30). Listen to music while munching on New York-style pizza and scrumptious brownies made with chocolate from the nearby plantation. American expat owner Alan Slesinger also organizes excursions to his nearby cocoa farm.

Most of Bahia's best cocoa has been exported, but you can get a sublime taste of the homegrown product at ★ Itacaré Cacau (Praça Santos Dumont 16, tel. 73/3251-3349, http://itacarecacau.com, 1pm-10pm daily), where local chocolate maker Maria Joanita sells artisanally crafted cocoa liqueurs and truffles (including a to-die-for version filled with cucuaçu jelly and cashews).

Transportation and Services

Itacaré has no tourist office, but it does have a terrific English and Portuguese bilingual website, www.itacare.com. There's a Bradesco ATM that accepts international cards, but no banks, so stock up on cash.

Itacaré is 70 kilometers (43 mi) north of Ilhéus along highway BA-001. Ilhéus's airport has daily flights from Salvador, Porto Seguro, and São Paulo. Rota (tel. 73/3251-2181, www.rotatransportres.com.br) offers hourly buses 5am-7:45pm from Ilhéus. The 90-minute trip costs R$12, and the bus station (tel. 73/3251-2200) is only a short distance from the center. A taxi to your hotel costs R$15; a wheelbarrow taxi costs R$7. Or take a taxi from Ilhéus (usually the airport); most hotels have their own trusted drivers, or you can contact PC Taxi (tel. 73/3086-3072, R$150). It's also possible to reach Itacaré from Salvador via BA-001, heading south from Bom Despacho on the island of Itaparica. From Bom Despacho, Águia Branca (tel. 71/4004-1010, www.aguiabranca.com.br) and Cidade Sol (tel. 71/3682-1791, www.viacaocidadesol.com.br) provide a half-dozen daily bus departures (4 hours, R$40).

ILHÉUS

Ilhéus is the main city along what's known as Brazil's Cocoa Coast. The town dates back to the early 1500s; during colonial times, it thrived due to the sugarcane trade. Its true boom came in the late 19th-century with the introduction of *cacau* (cocoa) by Jesuits from the Amazon. Plummeting world prices and the abolition of slavery caused the sugar plantations to go into decline. However, cocoa—which earned the nickname *ouro branco* (white gold)—drew freed slaves and entrepreneurs to the hills surrounding Ilhéus, all of them seized by the desire to strike it rich (or at least earn a decent living). A handful of cocoa barons (known as *coronéis*, or colonels), with vast plantations, did indeed become immensely wealthy and powerful. They ruled over their workers and the region as a whole until the 1980s, when a fungus known as *vassoura de bruxa* ("witch's broom") decimated the cocoa trees and left the region's economy in ruins, from which it has only recently begun to recuperate. Today, traces of the legacy of the "colonels" can be glimpsed by wandering among the handful of grandiose mansions and civic buildings of Ilhéus's small historical center. You can also read about their exploits in the novels (particularly *The Violent Land*) of famous Brazilian author Jorge Amado (1912-2001), Ilhéus's most illustrious son. The loss in revenue from cocoa has been somewhat offset by the development of tourism. Ilhéus is surrounded by native Atlantic forest and, to the north and south, it boasts attractive white-sand beaches—all of which make it well worth exploring.

Sights

Ilhéus's tiny historical center makes for a pleasant morning or afternoon stroll. Many of its landmarks have become renowned throughout Brazil due to their presence in Jorge Amado's novels. On Praça Luiz Viana Fialho, the Teatro Municipal, built in 1932, was formerly a cinema where an adolescent Amado frequently went to watch movies. On a corner of the square, the Casa de Cultura

Jorge Amado (Rua Jorge Amado 21, tel. 73/3634-8986, 9am-noon and 2pm-6pm Mon.-Fri., 9am-noon Sat., R\$4) is housed in the family mansion, built by the author's father in 1920 after he struck it rich with a winning lottery ticket; guided tours are offered. Nearby, the Praça J. J. Seabra, Praça Rui Barbosa, and Rua Antônio Lavigne contain early 20th-century homes and palaces that attest to the wealth of the cocoa barons. Built in 1534, the Igreja de São Jorge on Praça Rui Barbosa is Ilhéus's oldest church, while the towering mid-20th-century Catedral de São Sebastião, on Praça Dom Eduardo, displays an unusual blend of architectural styles.

There are still cocoa plantations in operation near Ilhéus. Since cocoa trees require shade to grow, farms preserve many taller tree specimens of native Atlantic forest, which makes a stroll through these estates a pleasurable outing. Visitors can taste the cocoa and sample the succulent nectar made from its fruit. Fazenda Yrerê (tel. 73/3656-5054, R\$25) is 11 kilometers (7 mi) from town on highway BR-415, which links Ilhéus to Itabuna. Another 9 kilometers (6 mi) out of Ilhéus on the same road is Fazenda Primavera (tel. 73/3231-3996, R\$20). Advance reservations are necessary. Trips can be organized through Órbita Turismo e Expedições (Rua Fernando Leite Mendes 71, tel. 73/3234-3250, www.orbitaexpedicoes. com.br), which offers city tours as well as outings to hidden beaches, waterfalls, forest reserves, and a sloth rehabilitation center.

Beaches

The beaches within Ilhéus are neither very clean nor appealing; most locals head north toward Itacaré or to the beaches south of the city. After Praia do Sul, one of the closest and most popular is Praia dos Milionários. Only 7 kilometers (4.5 mi) from the center of town, its name alludes to its past as the favored beach of Ilhéus's wealthy cocoa barons. You don't have to be rich to sit at the many barracas along this coconut-shaded beach.

Wilder, more enticing beaches include Praia de Cururupe, along with Backdoor and Batuba, both in the vicinity of Olivença, a little fishing village 16 kilometers (10 mi) from Ilhéusare. Large waves make swimming dangerous, though they attract surfers. Backdoor is a well-kept secret of hardcore surfers, who worship its exceptionally long point breaks. Another well-kept secret is Olivença's natural hot springs; its medicinal properties are claimed to not only hydrate and rejuvenate skin, but leave you with a tan. Municipal buses serve all these beaches and depart at 30-minute intervals between 6pm-10pm from the local rodoviári.

Accommodations

While hotels in the center of Ilhéus are usually good bargains, they tend to be older and not in mint condition; a handful retain some historical character. The Ilhéus Hotel (Rua Eustáquio Bastos 144, tel. 73/3634-4242, www.ilheushotel.com.br, R\$80-180 d) is a case in point. Inaugurated in 1930, the block-long hotel was the brainchild of one of the area's richest cocoa barons, who dreamed of building the most modern and luxurious hotel in all of Bahia. At the time, his architectural plans consisted of such novelties as separate bathrooms for men and women, as well as the state's first elevator, still in operation today. Long since overhauled, the guest rooms are modern and modest, but stylish remnants of its glory days compensate.

Beach bums, nature buffs, and getaway artists will find refuge along the still-wild coastline north of Ilhéus. ★ Casa Paraíso Verde (Rod. BA-001 km 30, tel. 73/9971-7371, www.casaparaisoverde.com.br, R\$275-500 d; add R\$100 pp full-board) is located 30 kilometers (19 mi) north of Ilhéus amidst a tangle of rain forest that is truly a "verdant paradise." Owned by American artist Kenny Scharf and his Ilhéus-born wife, Tereza, the quintet of beautifully crafted treehouse style eco-bungalows is a homey retreat. Back in the '80s, close friend Keith Haring created several art installations on the premises. Just a short walk away are waterfalls and deserted, palmed-lined beaches ideal for endless shelling, bathing, and surfing. Back at the *casa*, indulge in a yoga session, watch a film, or relax in a breeze-swung hammock.

Food

On Praia dos Milionários, Armação (tel. 73/3632-1817, 8am-5pm daily, R$20-30) offers delicious fish and seafood as well as heady Bahian *moquecas*. In town, an Ilhéus classic is Bar Vesúvio (Praça Dom Eduardo 190, tel. 73/3634-2164, www.barvesuvio.com.br, 10am-midnight Mon.-Sat., 6pm-midnight Sun., R$25-40). Built in 1919, it appeared in several of Jorge Amado's novels and is a local institution. The menu is a mix of Arab and Bahian specialties. Take a seat at one of the sidewalk tables, order a beer, and engage in some people-watching; live music is played nightly.

Information and Services

Tourist information is available at the *rodoviária* and the airport. Bahiatursa (Rua Estáquio Bastos 308, tel. 73/3231-8679, 7:30am-5pm Mon.-Fri.) and Setur (Av. Soares Lopes 1741, tel. 73/3634-6008, www.ilheusdabahia.tur.br) are both located in the historic center. A good Portuguese and English website is www.brasilheus.com.br. A convenient Banco do Brasil ATM that accepts international cards is near the cathedral (Rua Marquês de Paranaguá 112).

Transportation

The Aeroporto Jorge Amado (tel. 73/3234-4000) is 4 kilometers (2.5 mi) south from the center of town and close to the beaches south of the city. There are daily flights to Ilhéus from Salvador, Porto Seguro, Rio de Janeiro, and São Paulo. The long-distance *rodoviária* (tel. 73/3634-4121), in Pontal, is also only 4 kilometers (2.5 mi) west from the center and easily accessible by taxi or municipal bus. Águia Branca (tel. 71/4004-1010, www.aguiabranca.com.br) operates numerous daily buses from Salvador's *rodoviária* (7 hours, R$70-170) and two a day (at 9am and

1pm from Bom Despacho (5.5 hours, R$46). Rota (tel. 73/3634-3161, www.rotatransportres.com.br) has four daily connections to Porto Seguro (five hours, R$50-67). Driving to Ilhéus from either the north or south, take BR-101 to Itabuna, and then take coastal BR-415 for 40 kilometers (25 mi) to Ilhéus.

TO CANAVIEIRAS

The pretty little colonial town of Canavieiras, located 120 kilometers (68 mi) south of Ilhéus, has a surprisingly well-preserved historic center with candy-colored mansions built by local sugar and cocoa barons. There are deserted beaches as well as mangrove swamps, where you can treat yourself to a mud bath. The surrounding coastline is one of the best places for blue marlin fishing; the mighty fish can measure up to 5 meters (16 feet) in length and 500 kilograms (1,100 pounds) in weight; for this reason, landing one is a true battle. Bahia Pesca Esportiva (tel. 11/3284-1137, www.bahiapescaesportiva.com.br) organizes fishing trips. A day of marlin fishing costs R$3,800 for four people. To spend the night, the German-owned Bahiadomizil (Av. Beira Mar 1065, tel. 73/3284-2902, www.bahiadomizil.com, R$120-180 d) offers a quintet of laid-back beach bungalows beneath the palms with kitchens and living rooms. Cidade Sol (tel. 73/3231-3392, www.viacaocidadesol.com.br) operates 10 daily buses from Ilhéus to Canavieiras (2.5 hours, R$20). For more information, check out www.canavieiras-ba.com.br.

PORTO SEGURO

When you arrive in Porto Seguro, you'll be greeted by banners touting the fact that this is where Brazil "began." Indeed, Porto's claim to fame as the nation's first city stems from the fact that it was here in 1500 that Brazil's "discoverer," Pedro Alves Cabral, planted his wooden cross in the name of the Portuguese crown. Half a millennium later, Porto Seguro is better known as the birthplace of the 1980s dance craze known as the *lambada* and as one of the biggest and most ballyhooed beach resorts in all of Brazil. Indeed, despite a few colonial vestiges and some attractive beaches, Porto Seguro is all about packing in the tourists. Synonymous with two words, *package tour,* in the summertime, the place is downright Floridian in its touristic fervor as Brazilian families check into condos and crowds of young party animals crash in fleabag hotels after drinking and dancing the night away. As a party capital, Porto is known for two merrymaking institutions: the Passarela do Alcool, or "Alcohol Catwalk," a seaside promenade filled with stands hawking near-explosive fruit cocktails, and sprawling, sophisticated beach bars known as "mega-barracas": By day they function like fully equipped adult playgrounds, while at night they metamorphose into raucous clubs that are home to luaus and raves. Although Porto's heyday has passed, leaving the place a little beat-up and seedy around the edges, if you want to party hearty—and then nurse your hangover on some fine beaches—this is the place to be. However, those seeking something with more natural beauty and charm are best advised to take a quick look around and then head north to Santo André or south to Arraial d'Ajuda, Trancoso, and lovelier points further down the coast.

Sights

Perched strategically on a verdant bluff overlooking the ocean, the handful of colonial buildings that compose Porto Seguro's *centro histórico* mark the beginning of Brazil's official history. A five-minute walk from the *rodoviária* or a fast but steep climb up a staircase from the main traffic circle at the end of Avenida 22 de Abril is all it takes to rewind time a few centuries. A couple of hours can be easily spent—with or without the guidance of eager (and expensive) local guides—wandering among the pastel-painted houses and gleaming churches. Arrive early in the morning when the light is golden or in the late afternoon to catch the sunset.

Begin at the foot of Brazil's oldest monument, the Marco da Posse. Brought over from Portugal in 1503, this marble column, worshipfully encased in glass, is tattooed with the insignia of the Portuguese crown and the cross of the Order of Christ. In the lovely Praça Pero de Campos Tourinho, the simple Igreja de Nossa Senhora da Penha (9am-noon and 2pm-5pm daily) dates back to 1535 and boasts an impressive icon of São Francisco de Assis. In the same green square is the Casa de Câmara e Cadeia, the former town hall and Brazil's first public jail. Today, its polished interior houses the small Museu de Porto Seguro (tel. 73/3288-5182, 9am-5pm Tues.-Sun. and daily Jan.-Feb., R$6), with a collection of maps and indigenous artifacts. Nearby, in the Praça da Misericórdia, stands the Igreja de Nossa Senhora da Misericórdia. Built in 1526, it is the oldest church in Brazil. Among the treasures inside its modest Museu de Arte Sacra (9am-5pm Tues.-Sun., R$2) are a ruby-encrusted statue of Senhor dos Passos and a life-size Christ on the crucifix, both dating from the late 16th century. More understated is the tiny, whitewashed Igreja São Benedito (1549), which now lies in atmospheric ruins.

Beaches

Porto Seguro's beach culture is concentrated on the 20 kilometers (12.5 mi) of low scrub and palm-flanked coastline that spread north from the city center. As far as urban beaches go, you could do a lot worse. The sand is sugary and white and the water, protected by reefs, is not only child-friendly but comes in unreal shades of jade and aqua. The Curuípe, Itacimirim, Mundaí, Taperapuã, Ponta Grande, and Mutá beaches reach up from Porto to Coroa Vermelha, 13 kilometers (8 mi) to the north. The first few are packed with *barracas,* including the famous mega-barracas that are entertainment complexes. By day, these offer *lambada* and *"lambaérobica"* classes, water sports, and Internet access as well as food and drink. By night, their multiple stages host musical performers and DJs that whip the crowd into a sweat to the throbbing strains of *axé, forró,* pop, and techno.

Porto Seguro

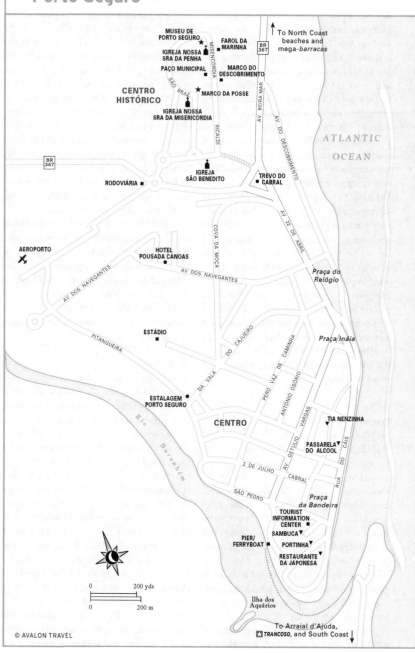

MUSEU DE PORTO SEGURO

FAROL DA MARINHA

IGREJA NOSSA SRA DA PENHA

PAÇO MUNICIPAL

MARCO DO DESCOBRIMENTO

To North Coast beaches and mega-*barracas*

BR 367

MISERICÓRDIA

CENTRO HISTÓRICO

MARCO DA POSSE

SÃO BRAZ

IGREJA NOSSA SRA DA MISERICORDIA

ATLANTIC OCEAN

RICALDI

AV BEIRA MAR

AV DO DESCOBRIMENTO

BR 367

IGREJA SÃO BENEDITO

RODOVIÁRIA

TREVO DO CABRAL

COVA DA MOCA

AV 22 DE ABRIL

AEROPORTO

HOTEL POUSADA CANOAS

AV DOS NAVEGANTES

Praça do Relógio

AV DOS NAVEGANTES

PITANGUEIRA

ESTÁDIO

DO CAJUEIRO

PERO VAZ DE CAMINHA

Praça Inãia

DA VALA

ANTÔNIO OSÓRIO

ESTALAGEM PORTO SEGURO

CENTRO

VARGAS

DO CAIS

TIA NENZINHA

AV GETÚLIO

PASSARELA DO ALCOOL

2 DE JULHO

CABRAL

RUA

SÃO PEDRO

Praça da Bandeira

TOURIST INFORMATION CENTER

PIER/ FERRYBOAT

SAMBUCA

PORTINHA

RESTAURANTE DA JAPONESA

Rio Buranhém

0   200 yds

0   200 m

Ilha dos Aquários

To Arraial d'Ajuda, TRANCOSO, and South Coast

© AVALON TRAVEL

The biggest, loudest, and hippest of these are Tôa-Tôa (Av. Beira Mar km 5, Taperapuã, tel. 73/3679-1714, www.portaltoatoa.com), Axé Moi (Av. Beira Mar 6500, Taperapuã, tel. 73/3679-1248, www.axemoi.com.br), and the granddaddy of them all, Barramares (Av. Beira Mar km 68.5, Taperapuã, tel. 73/3679-2980, www.barramares.com.br). More sedate is the relatively distant beach of Mutá. From the traffic circle in the center of town, municipal buses go north along to coast to the sleepy town of Santa Cruz de Cabrália. At night, you're better off taking a cab.

Entertainment and Events
NIGHTLIFE

Porto Seguro's sizzling nightlife begins in town along the legendary Passarela do Alcool, an ultratouristy and pretty garish seaside promenade of bars, restaurants, and hundreds of stands hawking tacky T-shirts, "indigenous" trinkets, and the potent local cocktail, *capeta*. This is both an energizing and intoxicating potion made from pure cocoa powder, Amazonian jolt-providing *guaraná* powder, vodka, sugar, and ice. As a final touch, sweet condensed milk is added to make the medicine go down nice and easy. The many drink stands along the Passarela—most of them more flamboyantly decked out than a Carmen Miranda tutti-frutti hat—also serve up everything from caipirinhas to *batidas* mixed with *cachaça* and fresh fruit.

The Passarela serves as a warm-up for the nightly extravaganzas held at the mega-*barracas* along the northern beaches of Mundaí and Taperapuã as well as Ilha dos Aquários (Ilha do Pacuico, access from Praça do Pataxó, tel. 73/3268-2828, www.ilhadosaquarios.com.br), located on a private island in the Rio Buranhém; its attractions include various immense aquariums filled with glitzy fish. Each *barraca* (some operate during normal business hours) has its own *festa* night (widely advertised by fliers along the Passarela). The weekday action is more exciting than on the weekends; bear in mind that it's all geared to young Brazilian party animals. Free buses usually head up and down the coast from the traffic circle off Avenida 22 de Abril. The cover for most shows is R$30-60.

FESTIVALS AND EVENTS

Porto Seguro's summer festivities come to a head during Carnaval. Although much smaller than Salvador's celebration, the *axé*-throbbing merrymaking lasts for a lot longer—until the Saturday following Ash Wednesday. This gives Salvador's megastars a chance to migrate south and whip the party into full swing. A more traditional celebration is the Festa de São Benedito (Dec. 25-27), held in the *centro histórico,* in which traditional African music and dances are performed.

Accommodations

Accommodation options range from very basic closet-size rooms to megaresorts dripping with amenities. Off-season coincides with high vacancies and discounts galore, but as early as October things starting going up, and by December even the prices of fleabags will have doubled. During New Year's and Carnaval, prices are astronomical, and throughout the summer, it's best to make reservations. Prices below are for off-season.

If you are happy with the simple combination of a bed and clean digs, there are many choices, although these budget *pousadas* are very tiny, often dark and a bit musty, and devoid of any decorative scheme. One of the nicer inexpensive options is Hotel Pousada Canoas (Av. Navegantes, tel. 73/3288-2205, pousadahotelcanoas.jimdo.com, R$100-140 d). The small but Spartan whitewashed guest rooms with wooden accents have basic amenities including cable TV and air conditioning and are clustered around a garden with a swimming pool. Its prime location is close to all the action. Overlooking the Rio Buranhém, Estalagem Porto Seguro (Rua Marechal Deodoro 66, tel. 73/3288-2095, www.hotelestalagem.com.br, R$100 pp, R$80-170 d) is simple but atmospheric. Housed in a 200-year-old inn once frequented by traveling cocoa barons, the building's original walls were constructed out of stone and whale oil; ceiling beams of brazil wood are still apparent. Rooms in the new wing are less charming, but compensate with verandas hung with hammocks and a small pool.

Food

Amidst the tourist traps in central Porto, there are a handful of surprisingly good eateries to choose from. A culinary touchstone, Tia Nenzinha (Pássarela do Alcool 170, tel. 73/3288-1846, noon-midnight Tues.-Sun. and daily from Dec.-Feb., R$20-30) has been dishing up *moquecas* and other traditional Bahian fish and seafood dishes since the mid-1970s. Sugar fiends can top off their meal with a succulently moist *cocadas* (freshly grated coconut and sugar mixed with honey, chocolate, or guava). The best pizza in town is in a pretty coral-colored house with a cozy white interior called Sambuca (Praça dos Pataxós 216, tel. 73/3288-2366, 6pm-midnight daily, R$20-30), located right beside the pier. Directly opposite, Restaurante da Japonesa (Praça dos Pataxós 38, tel. 73/3288-5606, 7am-midnight daily, R$20-40) possesses an eclectic menu—everything from Bahian *moqueca* and Portuguese *bacalhau* to cheeseburgers and chop suey. The sushi and sashimi are made with fresh fish locally caught by Ju—reputed to be the Discovery Coast's one and only sushiwoman—and are excellent (and reasonably priced). A small emporium on the premises is a great place to load up on Japanese snacks. For cheap, fast, and delicious *comida por quilo*, head to Portinha (Rua Saldanha Marinha 43, tel. 73/3288-2743, www.portinha.com.br, noon-5pm and 6pm-10pm daily, R$15-20). Pick and choose from a mouthwatering buffet of fresh salads and hot dishes warmed over a wood oven, then savor your meal at wooden picnic tables in the leafy garden or out on the cobblestoned street.

Transportation and Services

There are tourist offices at the *rodoviária* and at Praça Manoel Ribeiro Coelho 10 (on the Passarela do Alcool, 9am-11pm Mon.-Sat.). International bank cards are accepted at the Banco do Brasil and HSBC ATMs in the center of town.

There are usually numerous and often inexpensive (if booked in advance) flights available to Porto Seguro from Rio, São Paulo, and Salvador. The international airport (Estrada do Aeroporto 1500, tel. 73/3288-1880) is a five-minute taxi ride from the city center.

Buses from all over Brazil also serve Porto. Águia Branca (tel. 73/3288-1039, www.aguiabranca.com.br), whose night bus has reclining sleepers, offers two daily buses north to Salvador (11 hours, R$150). São Geraldo (tel. 73/3288-1198, www.saogeraldo.com.br) has one daily bus to Rio (19 hours, R$186). The *rodoviária* (tel. 73/3288-1914) is a five-minute taxi or bus ride to the center of town.

If you're traveling by car, turn off BR-101 at Eunápolis and take the Porto Seguro turnoff (BR-367) for roughly 70 kilometers (43 mi).

North of Porto Seguro

North along the coast from Porto Seguro, the beaches become more deserted and unspoiled. From Santa Cruz de Cabrália, 25 kilometers (16 mi) north, a boat trip across the Rio João de Tiba brings you to the rustic and surprisingly undervisited fishing settlement of Santo André (www.santoandrebahia.com). Santo André's long coastline of empty beaches and swaying palms makes a nice antidote to Porto's urban beach scene. Farther north, you'll hit the surfer's paradise of Guaiú and Mojiquiçaba, followed by the atmospherically decaying town of Belmonte, with its faded mansions once owned by cocoa barons. To stay a while in Santo André, there are a handful of *pousadas,* although no banks or gas stations. Pousada Ponta de Santo André (Rua Beira-Rio, tel. 73/3671-4031, www.stoandre.com.br, R$150-235 d) is a pleasant riverside option with tropically rustic apartments and bungalows set amid greenery. Guests can take advantage of kayaks, sailboats, and windsurfers.

From Santa Cruz de Cabrália, ferries (tel.

73/3282-1094) leave every half-hour from the port; the 10-minute crossing costs R$1 for pedestrians and R$11 for cars. Buses operated by Expresso Brasileiro (tel. 73/3288-3650, www.expressobrasileiro.com.br) travel from Porto Seguro's airport and bus terminal at 20-minute intervals to Santo Cruz (R$4.40) between 5am-midnight and from the far side of the river to Santo André at hourly intervals between 6:30am-7:15pm (R$2.50).

ARRAIAL D'AJUDA

Despite being only a 10-minute boat ride across the Rio Buranhém from Porto Seguro, Arraial is another world. A major tourist destination in its own right, the town is much more charming than Porto. Aside from its splendid beaches, Arraial's winding streets, shaded by lofty trees and overflowing with atmospheric bars and restaurants, give off a pleasurable vibe that proves quite addictive. While Arraial boasts a Central Park and its main downtown drag is known as Rua da Broadway (or "Bróduei," as it's spelled locally), much more in keeping with New York City is the town's cosmopolitan air and edible fare. Both can be sampled on the Rua do Mucugê, a bustling artery lined with boutiques, bars, and restaurants that magically springs to life come sundown. Proof of how international this thoroughfare has become is in the number of multilingual menus and the 24-hour Internet cafés touting Hebrew keyboards. Indeed, in the summer, Arraial can get as packed as Porto, although the crowd is more alternative and upscale, as are the parties. Most of these all-night affairs are luaus or raves that take place at the sophisticated barracas and in the surrounding white sands of Mucugê and Parracho beaches. During the off-season, however, the town is deliciously tranquil. Although it was founded in the early 16th century, aside from the pretty Igreja Matriz de Nossa Senhora de Ajuda, built on a cliff and offering stunning views of the beaches below, there are few remnants of its colonial past. However, the present is certainly inviting.

Beaches

A quick and steep descent down the Rua do Mucugê will bring you right onto the soft white sands of Arraial's closest beach, Praia do Mucugê. If you turn left, you will pass Apaga-Fogo, lined with pousadas, from which you can rent equipment for water-sports activities such as kayaking and windsurfing. More popular with locals than tourists is tranquil Araçaipe, which has some great beach bars. Turning right will take you past the trendy Praia do Parracho, with its many barracas, to the startlingly beautiful Praia da Pitinga, whose sugary sands are backed by jagged red and white stone cliffs. Continuing onward, you'll reach the equally beautiful and deserted Praia de Taípe, where sunbathing in the nude is de rigueur. During low tide you can continue on to Trancoso, a 12-kilometer (7.5-mi) stroll, then take a bus back.

Sports and Recreation

Arco Íris Turismo (Rua do Mucugê 199, tel. 73/3575-1672) offers full-day outings in which a van picks you up at your hotel and takes you to the sublime beaches of Praia de Espelho and Trancoso (R$50) or Praia do Espelho and Caraíva (R$55). Other fun ways of exploring the coastline are by quadricycle or on horseback. Bahia Eco Adventure (tel. 73/3575-8568, www.bahiaeco.com) organizes half-day quadricycle outings (R$150 per vehicle) for small groups to Praia de Taípe as well as full-moon nocturnal outings that include a luau on the beach. The Centro Equestre (Praia dos Pescadores, tel. 73/3575-3965) offers several excursions on horseback, both on the beach and in the native Atlantic forest (R$70 for 90 minutes). You can also rent a bike (R$35 a day) at Arraial Trip Tur (tel. 73/3575-2805, www. arraialtriptur.com.br).

Although the coral reefs make for safe swimming on most of these beaches, it may be hard to resist the aquatic options at Arraial d'Ajuda Eco Parque (Estrada da Balsa Km 4.5, tel. 73/3575-8600, www.arraialecoparque. com.br, 10am-5pm Thurs.-Fri. and daily in

Jan., closed May-June, adults R$85), located on Praia do Mucugê. Supposedly the biggest water park in Latin America, its attractions include a wave pool, twisting water slides, and rappelling and tree-climbing in the jungle.

Between July and October, humpback whales are busy mating and giving birth along the Bahian coast. To see the great mammals in action, Cia do Mar (tel. 73/3575-2495) offers five-hour outings (R$150), departing from the *balsa,* in the company of a marine biologist.

Accommodations

The vast majority of accommodation options in Arraial are quite enticing. Prices are reasonable in the off-season, but come summertime, they can double and you'll need to reserve in advance. Rates listed are for off-season.

One of Arraial's nicest affordable options is the Tubarão Pousada (Rua Bela Vista 210, tel. 73/3575-3379, www.pousada-tubaraoarraial.com, R$60-90 d). On a pretty cobblestoned cul-de-sac, facing a cliff with stupendous beach views, the hotel offers pleasant, guest rooms that open onto a shady oasis with a pool. Also a good bargain is the attractive Hotel Pousada Saudosa Maloca (Alameda da Eugênias 31, tel. 73/2105-1200, www.saudosamaloca.tur.br, R$180-230 d). Located on a tranquil sandy street, its modern guest rooms with verandas and swinging hammocks overlook a garden with a pool and a cheery breakfast area. Its more recently constructed neighbor, Hostel Maloca (Alameda da Eugênias 10, tel. 73/3575-1473, www.maloca.hostel.br, R$115-180 d, R$40-50 pp), offers a budget version with basic, spotless dorms and private rooms. Amenities include a cool pool, plenty of greenery, and delicious breakfasts. Pousada Bucaneiros (Rua do Mucugê 590, tel. 73/3575-1105, www.pousadabucaneiros.com.br, R$120-160 d) has a terrific location only two minutes from Mucugê beach. Although tightly packed within a garden complex, the simple guest rooms harbor a beach house vibe, enhanced with warm decorative touches. The friendly owners can organize

walking trips and excursions. Three bungalows come with fully equipped kitchens and are ideal for families or big groups. For sublime sea views, go across the street, where the massive windows and generous verandas of the tropically swank Hotel Paraíso do Morro (Rua do Mucugê 471, tel. 73/3575-3330, www.paraisodomorro.com, R$320-380 d) will leave you gasping in awe. Other standouts include a beckoning pool and attentive service. Those seeking a home-away-from-home will find it at ★ Casa Natureza (Rua dos Coqueiros 27, tel. 73/3575-10701, www.casanaturezabrasil.com.br, R$176-220 d). Reni Azevedo transformed his family's abode in the leafy residential *bairro* of São Francisco into a welcoming B&B. Four beautifully furnished suites spread between two villas are equipped with living areas, a kitchen, and even a yoga room. The jungly grounds include a pool as well as myriad monkeys.

Pousada Pitinga (Praia de Pitinga, tel. 73/3575-1067, www.pousadapitinga.com.br, no children under age 12, closed May-June, R$390-590 d) is set in a lush jungle area that spills right onto the sand. Tropically chic guest rooms rely on raw and polished natural materials, lulling you into a state of total harmony with nature. There is a pool for lounging. For a loftier, more removed vision of Arraial's seascapes, ★ Casarão Alto do Mucugê (Estrada Alto Mucugê 17, tel. 73/3575-1490, www.casaraoaltomucuge.com, R$230-350 d) features eight appealingly rustic guest rooms divided between a main house (*casarão*) and bungalows dispersed throughout a garden. Perched upon a cliff overlooking Praia de Pitinga, the intoxicating views and soundtrack of crashing waves are constant companions. Enjoy a lavish al fresco breakfasts or sunset-watching from the Japanese hot tub. Despite the seclusion, it's only a five-minute walk to the center of town.

Food

By day, beach *barracas* also offer all sorts of fish, seafood, and other beach-worthy delicacies that can assuage hunger pangs of all sizes throughout the day. Especially good are Barraca do Nel (Praia dos Pescadores, tel. 73/3575-2816, 10am-5pm daily) and the sophisticatedly loungey Flor do Sal (Praia de Pitinga, tel. 73/3575-3078, 9am-5pm Tues.-Sun. Mar.-Nov. and daily Dec.-Feb.), whose options bear a distinctive Thai influence.

In Arraial, most restaurant kitchens don't get going until the end of the day. When they do, the options are very eclectic. Bahian food is the exception among the sushi bars, Italian cantinas, Argentinean steak houses, and other international eateries (concentrated on the Rua do Mucugê). When you can't take any more fish or seafood, Boi nos Aires (Rua do Mucugê 200, tel. 73/3575-2554, www.boinosairesrestaurante.com, 5pm-midnight daily, R$25-45) will have you back in carnivore heaven with its prime cuts of beef flown in from Buenos Aires (although it does grill fish as well). Manguti (Rua do Mucugê 99, tel. 73/3575-2270, www.manguti.com.br, noon-11pm daily, R$35-50) is another local favorite that serves up meat, fish, pasta, and its famous gnocchi in a variety of sauces. The setting, in a cozy little house that is slightly removed from Rua do Mucugê's buzz, is quite romantic. You've never seen a food court quite as fetching as the Beco das Cores, an open-air galleria that groups together a series of bewitchingly lit boutiques, bars, and restaurants serving everything from crepes and pizza to sushi. An alluring ambiance is also one of the attractions of ★ Rosa dos Ventos (Alameda dos Flamboyants 24, tel. 73/3575-1271, 4pm-midnight Mon.-Tues. and Thurs.-Sat. and daily Dec.-Feb., 1pm-10pm Sun. Mar.-Nov., R$50-60), located in a gracious house lit by candles and surrounded by tropical foliage. The surprising menu pairs tropical dishes such as fish baked in banana leaves with wonderfully rich Viennese desserts.

For less expensive sustenance, brave the lineups (in summer) at Paulo Pescador (Praça São Brás 116, tel. 73/3575-1242, noon-10pm Tues.-Sun. and daily Dec.-Feb., closed May, R$15-25). The simple Bahian fish dishes rely on fresh ingredients at this unassuming local eatery in the main square, a great vantage point for watching the hippies selling their wares at the nightly craft market. Nearby, in a chalet-style house looking onto "Central Park," is the pioneering per-kilo restaurant Portinha (Rua do Campo, tel. 73/3575-1289, www.portinha.com.br, noon-10pm daily, R$10-15). Like its siblings in Porto Seguro and Trancoso, the buffets feature a tasty assortment of varied salads and main dishes kept hot over a wood oven.

To satisfy sweet cravings, head to the charming Praça Brigadeiro Eduardo Gomes. Café da Santa (Rua Brigadeiro Eduardo Gomes 134, tel. 73/3575-1078, 7am-10pm Tues.-Sun.) serves delicious, freshly ground coffee along with plenty of pastries (including flaky croissants).

Transportation and Services

Many hotels have tourist information about Arraial, as does the tourist office in Porto Seguro and a small but well-stocked kiosk at the beginning of Rua Mucugê. You can also check out the Portuguese website www.arraialdajuda.tur.br. The local Bradesco ATM on the Praça São Braz accepts international cards.

Balsas (ferries) leave from Porto Seguro to Arraial at 30-minute intervals throughout the day. After midnight, they leave at hourly intervals. Round-trip fare is R$4 for pedestrians, R$13 (weekdays)/R$20 (weekends) for cars. The *balsas*—some allow cars, while others are strictly for passengers—leave from Praça dos Pataxós in Porto Seguro. Tickets can be purchased at Rio Buranhém Navegação (tel. 73/3288-2516). Once you arrive at the other side of the river, buses, vans (R$3), and *moto-taxis* (R$6) transport you along the 6-kilometer (3.5-mi) coastal road to the center of Arraial d'Ajuda. A taxi from Porto Seguro's airport will cost close to R$100.

★ TRANCOSO

Only 12 kilometers (7.5 mi) south of Arraial is lovely Trancoso, an upscale yet not too developed former hippie haven whose magical vibe, beautiful surroundings, and eco-chic ethos is a magnet for Brazilian and international magnates, celebs, and jetsetters with money to burn and stress to alleviate. Instead of the hard-core partying that goes on at Porto Seguro and Arraial, pilgrims to Trancoso often prefer an evening of fine dining followed by drinks at the candlelit al fresco restaurants sprinkled around the Quadrado (although the surrounding beaches offer their share of hedonistic nocturnal activities, particularly when the moon is full).

The Quadrado (Square), an immense open-air plaza carpeted in thick grass and framed by trees, is the historical, spiritual, and nerve center of Trancoso. On three sides, it is surrounded by colonial homes painted in vibrant colors, many of which now house stylish boutiques, *pousadas,* and restaurants. On the far side is the incandescent Igreja de São João Batista, built in the 18th century on the ruins of a Jesuit convent. As you approach the church, you also near the edge of the cliff behind it, which plummets down to a green tangle of native Atlantic forest, an endless strip of beach, and a great sweep of the Atlantic in shades of bright turquoise-green. The ensemble is intoxicating, and more than a little dreamlike.

Beaches

Only a five-minute descent from the Quadrado lie a series of gorgeous beaches, fed by rivers and bordered by mangrove swamps and rain forest-carpeted cliffs. At strategic intervals are funky *barracas* where you can catch the sun's rays while electronica, bossa nova and lounge music wafts through the air. Closest to Trancoso is Praias dos Nativos; the more deserted stretches attract the odd nudist. With calmer seas are the ultra-trendy Praia dos Coqueiros and Praia do Rio Verde, ideal for bathing. By horseback, buggy, or on foot, you can continue south along these primitive beaches, which stretch all the way to Caraíva.

Sports and Recreation

Natural Ecobike e Aventura (tel. 73/3668-1955, www.naturalecobike.com) operates excursions (R$150 for 2.5 hours) for various skill levels by day and at night. Another possibility is to go galloping down the beaches on horseback or kayaking down the crystalline waters of the Rio Trancoso to Praia dos Nativos, with stops for swimming. Trancoso Receptivo (tel. 73/3668-1183, www.trancoso-receptivo.com) charges R$150 for two hours of both pursuits. Golfers are in for a treat if

Trancoso

they choose to play the stunning 18-hole Terravista Gold Course (tel. 73/2105-2104, www.terravistagolfcourse.com.br, 8am-5pm Mon.-Sat., R$230 for 9 holes), located 18 kilometers (11 mi) from Trancoso on a cliff overlooking the Praia de Taípe.

Entertainment and Events

Trancoso's nightlife is less than wild, particularly in the off-season. There is usually a group playing live *forró*, samba, or rock music in the main square off the Quadrado or along the bars that lead down Rua Principal such as Para-Raio and São Brás, famed for its Friday night forró jams. In the summer, things heat up on the beaches of Praia dos Coqueiros and Praia do Rio Verde with parties, luaus, and even raves that last for days and draw a young, beautiful crowd. In summer, many of Trancoso's chicest hotels possess their own lounge barracas on Praia dos Nativos, among them Estrela d'Água, Uxua, and Bahia Bonita; all are open to the public.

Festa de São Sebastião (Jan. 20) is the town's most traditional *festa,* complete with processions, fireworks, and the raising of the two decorated masts that can be viewed in front of the church of São João Batista.

Accommodations

Trancoso's charming hotels tend to be on the pricy side, although some affordable options are available, particularly in and around the Bosque *bairro,* not far from the Quadrado. During the summer, prices double and reservations are a must. Prices listed are for off-season.

On the Quadrado, a lovely option is the Pousada Porto Bananas (Quadrado 234, tel. 73/3668-1017, www.portobananas.com.br, R$220-495 d). Various bungalows that sleep up to four are spread throughout a jungly garden that will make you feel as if you just checked into Eden. The tastefully simple guest rooms are decorated with harmonious colors and textures. You might find it hard to believe that there's anything but luxury on the Quadrado, but those on a budget can take refuge at the Albergue Café Esmeralda (Quadrado, tel. 73/3668-1527, www.trancosonatural.com, R$90-130 d). Although guest rooms are dark and cramped (only some have bathrooms), they are clean, and the owners are terribly friendly.

A little off the beaten track but also of great value is the Pousada Encantada (Rua João Vieira de Jesus, tel. 73/3668-2024, www.pousadaencantada.com.br, R$250-400 d). Although the bungalows are in close proximity and the garden is more residential backyard than tropical paradise, the guest rooms themselves are in mint condition and the staff makes you feel at home. Another fine choice, only 150 meters (500 feet) from the Quadrado, is the Pousada Mundo Verde (Rua João Vieira de Jesus, tel. 73/3668-2024, www.pousadamundoverde.com.br, R$220-310 d). The comfortable guest rooms aren't stylish, but the verdant surroundings are bucolic. From the pool at the edge of a bluff, you'll be treated to captivating views of the forest and beaches below.

There is no shortage of fabulous, eco-chic designer hotels in Trancoso. One of the first to rear its lovely head was ★ Etnia Pousada (Rua Principal 25, tel. 73/3668-1137, www.etniabrasil.com.br, R$510-630 d). This vast, hilly, and wooded property feels miles from the Quadrado. Immersed within the jungle are eight cleverly designed and beautifully appointed bungalows. Creature comforts include a humungous pool, terrace restaurant, and guests' access to the Etnia's private beach club on secluded Praia do Rio Verde. Located 2 kilometers south of town, Etnia Clube de Mar (Estrada Trancoso-Itaquena 300, tel. 73/3668-2065, www.etniaclubedemar.com.br, R$930-1,140 d) boasts a quintet of comfortable yet casual two-story beach houses ideal for couples and families in search of reclusion, relaxation, pampering, and privileged beach access. A hallmark of both Etnia properties is the extremely attentive service. If you have the urge to splurge, the most fabulous of Trancoso's accommodations options is ★ Uxua Casa (Quadrado, tel. 73/3668-2277, uxua.com, R$1,100-3,300 d)—the name, a Pataxó term for "marvelous," says it all. Dutch owner Wilbert Das applied his sensibility and impeccable taste to the 10 primitive bungalows (one is a treehouse), spread out beneath a canopy of native fruit trees. All were built using local construction techniques and recycled materials and are decorated with a captivating mélange of *artesanato* and antiques, as well as fixtures designed by Das himself. Open-sky bathrooms, full kitchens, private gardens, and indoor-outdoor living rooms make it hard to leave. The public spaces include a restaurant, lounge, and lagoon-shaped pool lined with 40,000 green aventurine quartz crystals supposed to possess healing properties. Uxua's beach club bar is made from recycled fishing boats. Service is superb yet casual and includes a 24-hour-personal concierge.

Food

Just as sophisticated as its accommodations are Trancoso's range of culinary choices. During the day, you can take advantage of the fare served at the beach *barracas*. One of the nicest is the Italian-owned ★ Cabana do Andrea on Praia de Coqueiros. The Italian salads and pizzas are flavorful, as are the more tropical selections, including shrimp cooked in coconut milk and served in a coconut and grilled shrimp and squid with mango chutney. The service is attentive and the mellow soundtrack will put you in a sweet trance, aided by beach chairs and hammocks galore.

The restaurant scene in town doesn't get hopping until sundown. One of the best options, day or night, is the per-kilo buffet at Portinha (Quadrado, tel. 73/3668-1054, www.portinha.com.br, noon-8pm daily Mar.-Dec., noon-10pm daily Jan.-Feb. and July, R$15-20). The deliciously fresh salads and hot dishes kept sizzling over a wood oven can be savored at picnic tables right on a tree-shaded patch of the Quadrado. Come sundown, if you don't want to repeat the experience, try another Quadrado favorite: Silvana & Cia (Quadrado, tel. 73/3668-1122,

1pm-10pm daily, R$40-50). Beneath a giant almond tree magically lit up with lanterns and candles, Trancoso-born Silvana prepares typical Bahian dishes such as grilled fish, shrimp *bobós*, and *moquecas*. It's nicely priced by Trancoso standards; locals often dine here.

Natives of both Italy and São Paulo (where pizza is king) swear by the crunchy pies prepared in the large open kitchen of Maritaca (Rua do Telégrafo 388, tel. 73/3668-1702, 7pm-11pm Tues.-Sun., 7pm-2am daily Jan.-Feb., R$25-35). The ambiance is casual, but toppings include the more refined likes of asparagus and brie. For a respite from Trancoso's lofty prices, head to Lá No Dom (Rua da Gameleira 43, 6pm-1am Mon.-Sat. and daily Jan.-Feb.), where Dom prepares robust pita sandwiches layered with his secret eggplant sauce.

Transportation and Services

Tourist information and reservations for excursions are available at Trancoso Receptivo (Rua Carlos Alberto Parracho, off the Quadrado, tel. 73/3688-1333, www.trancosoreceptivo.com). For information online, check out www.trancosobahia.com.br. Also on Rua Carlos Alberto Parracho are ATMs that accept international cards. In front is a taxi stand with service to surrounding destinations.

Hourly Águia Azul (tel. 73/3575-1175) buses run between Trancoso and the *balsa* at Arraial d'Ajuda from 6am-7pm. The 50-minute trip, most of it through papaya plantations, costs R$6. By car, follow the 38-kilometer (24-mi) Estrada Arraial-Trancoso. After 7 kilometers (4 mi), you can turn onto the Estrada Velha de Trancoso, a dirt road that is only 15 kilometers (9 mi) to Trancoso.

★ CARAÍVA

Off the beaten track—which has left it gloriously intact from developers—Caraíva is most people's fantasy of an idyllic tropical getaway. On the banks of the Rio Caraíva, this tiny fishing village is surrounded by the thick vegetation of mangroves as well as deserted white beaches that extend for kilometers in both directions. Its few roads are paved with silky sand instead of asphalt, which hardly matters since no cars exist here. You can hire a donkey-driven wooden chariot or jump into a dugout canoe to get around. After a 10-year battle with the national energy company, Caraíva finally received electricity in 2007. However, since residents are used to lanterns and candles, you'll still be able to wander around at night with little more than moonlight and starlight to guide you. There isn't much to do in Caraíva, but if all you want to do is completely relax in idyllic natural surroundings, it is incomparable.

Beaches

You can walk for hours along Caraíva's beautiful coastline, and there is barely any construction in sight to break the brilliant green of native Atlantic forest and swaying coconut palms. Going south from the Praia da Caraíva, the beaches will take you past the Parque Nacional Monte Pascoal (tel. 73/3288-1613, www.icmbo.gov.br, R$5), a nature preserve that is also partially occupied by the Barra Velha Pataxó reservation (guided excursions can be organized from Caraíva for R$40 pp for groups of eight), all the way down to the splendidly isolated beaches of Barra do Cai and Ponta do Corumbau, where there is wonderful diving.

Once you take a canoe across the Rio Caraíva, you can also make your way north along the coast. A 4-kilometer (2.5-mi) walk brings you to the Praia de Satu. Cutting into the red cliffs crowned with jungle are freshwater lagoons where you can swim. An alternative to walking is to hire a boat from the quays (R$20).

Day outings by boat (R$60) or high-speed *lanchas* (R$100-130) to beaches north or south of Caraíva depart from the quays along the river and include snorkels and masks to check out fish amidst the reefs; reserve in advance with *barqueiros* or at the Boteco da Pará. Also fun is taking a *lancha* or kayak up the Rio Caraíva and then spending 90 dreamy minutes floating back down the river in an inflated rubber tire.

Accommodations and Food

Caraíva hotels are pretty rustic, although they range from very basic to atmospheric. One of the most centrally located and attractive is ★ Pousada da Lagoa (tel. 73/3668-5059, www.lagoacaraiva.com.br, R$180-315 d). Brightly painted cabins are nestled among abundant foliage and around a small lagoon. The restaurant serves up nicely prepared meals (including garden-grown fruits and veg), and on summer nights it serves as bohemian headquarters to the mellow crowd that congregates to listen to great canned and live music. For immediate beach access, a nice option is the Pousada Casa da Praia (tel. 73/3274-6833, casadapraiacaraiva.com. br, R$180-270 d), which has a vast gazebo and lawn-chair studded garden as well as a lively bar. Guest rooms are simple but airy, with sea-facing verandas, and stepping outside means literally stepping into soft sand. The best bargain in town is Memoan Hostel (tel. 73/9275-7649, www.memoanhostel.com.br, R$70-100 d, R$35-40 pp), whose rustic dorm and double rooms (no TVs) are distributed amidst a spacious watermelon-colored *casa* surrounded by tropical gardens and overlooking the river. Guests are encouraged to cook in the communal kitchen and share the fruits of their labor at communal picnic tables.

Pará, the owner of ★ Boteco do Pará (Rua Beiro-Rio, tel. 73/9991-9804, 11am-6pm Tues.-Sun., 11am-10pm daily Dec.-Feb., R$20-35) has his own fishing boat, which guarantees the freshness of the fish and *moquecas* at this traditional eatery overlooking the Rio Caraíva. Tables are shaded by an immense almond tree and adjacent to the Ponto dos Mentirosos (Liars' Spot), where fishermen traditionally congregate to tell tall tales.

Transportation and Services

For information about Caraíva, check out www.caraiva.com.br. The Associação dos Nativos de Caraíva (near the church) offers contact info for local guides. Two buses daily (three daily in summer) operated by Águia Azul (tel. 73/3575-1175) connect Arraial d'Ajuda and Trancoso to Caraíva along a dirt road (that's difficult to navigate during the rainy season). The boat from Nova Caraíva to the village is R$4. From Arraial, the journey takes two hours and costs R$16. If you're driving, follow BR-101 to Monte Pascoal, then continue 42 kilometers (26 mi) along a dirt road to Nova Caraíva, where you'll have to leave your car.

Around Caraíva

Close to Caraíva are two of the most stunning and remote beaches along the Bahian coast: Praia do Espelho and Ponta do Corumbau. In recent years, despite (or because) of their seclusion, several rustically chic hotels have opened along their sands, allowing you to bed down in paradise—for a price.

PRAIA DO ESPELHO

With its coral-framed pools of limpid blue and flour-white beaches backed by dramatic red cliffs, it's no wonder that Praia do Espelho ranks at the top of the "Best Beaches" lists frequently compiled by Brazilian travel writers and hard-core beach aficionados. This means frequent boatloads of tourists show up from Porto Seguro and Arraial d'Ajuda. However, given Caraíva's 9-kilometer (6-mi) proximity, you can beat the crowds and enjoy the sheer beauty of the place in splendid isolation. An early arrival coincides with low tide. Reserve a boat from the Boteco do Pará (tel. 73/3274-6829); an outing costs R$60 and includes a stop at the Ilha de Tatuaçu for snorkeling. To stay a while and be pampered, a wonderful choice is ★ Hotel Fazenda Cala & Divino (tel. 73/9191-5183, www.divinoespelho.com.br, R$500-770 d). The former beach house of local ceramicist João José Calazans (a.k.a. Cala) boasts eight breezy guest chalets, beautifully decorated by the artist, that gaze out over the sea (you can even see the ocean from

bed). This is the only *pousada* with direct access to Praia do Espelho; others are located on the neighboring Praia do Curuipe. For a delicious lunch with a view, make advance reservations at Restaurante da Sylvinha (tel. 73/9985-4157, noon-3:30pm Mon.-Sat. Mar.-Nov., noon-6pm daily Dec.-Feb., R$50-65). Delicious fresh fish and seafood is prepared using regional fruits (mangaba, mango, passionfruit) and global influences (Moroccan, Thai, Mediterranean).

To get to Praia do Espelho from Arraial d'Ajuda, take the same Águia Azul (tel. 73/3575-1175, R$12.50) bus that goes to Caraíva, which will let you off at the entrance to town, 800 meters (0.5 mi) from the beach. By car, follow BR-101 to Monte Pascoal, and then continue 42 kilometers (26 mi) along a dirt road to Nova Caraíva; turn off at the sign indicating Praia do Espelho and then follow signed-turn offs to Praia do Espelho or to individual *pousadas*. If you plan to stay overnight, most *pousadas* can arrange transfers from Porto Seguro, Arraial, Trancoso, and Caraíva.

PONTA DO CORUMBAU

Corumbau remains one of the most unspoiled beaches along the Bahian coast. It's also one of the most alluring, with jade green water sheltered by coral reefs, a long white sand bar and endless beaches shaded by coconut palms and almond trees. From Caraíva, hire a boat at the Boteco do Pará to bring you here for the day (R$60, includes snorkel gear) or get Jonathan (tel. 73/9994-3371) or Nel (tel. 73/9901-8329) to zoom you here and back by buggy (R$150 for up to four people). To stay, ★ Vila Naia (tel. 73/3573-1006, www.vilanaia.com.br, R$1,400-1,800 d) is a stunning example of sustainable luxury. Four rustic fishermen's bungalows are scattered within a private reserve with trails that wind through mangroves and beaches, punctuated with wooden decks. Accommodations are comfortable and equipped with all modern amenities. There is also a spa with yoga classes, a pool, and an organic garden that supplies produce for delicious meals, included in the room rates. Much more affordable is Pousada Corumbau (tel. 73/3573-1190, www.corumbau.tur.br, R$150-290 d), which gives you a choice of apartments, bungalows, or an apartment with a kitchen and a living room. The clean, modern guest rooms are pretty modest, but the location is great, on a quasi-private strip of beach with its own *barraca*. Kids will love the hotel mascot: a large red macaw that wanders around as if he owns the place.

There is no bus service to Corumbau; driving takes forever and involves taking the BR-101 from the inland city of Itamaraju. The fastest and easiest way to get here is by boat or buggy via Caraíva.

CARAVELAS

Depending on which direction you're coming from, the last (or first) resort town of consequence in Bahia's extreme south is Caravelas. A decidedly low-key place, the colonial town's biggest draw is its proximity to the fantastic Parque Nacional Marinho de Abrolhos. Located 70 kilometers (43 mi) offshore, this marine reserve encompasses an archipelago of five islands whose crystalline waters and coral reefs make up one of the world's best diving spots.

★ Parque Nacional Marinho dos Abrolhos

Abrolhos comes from the Portuguese command *abre os olhos* ("open your eyes"), and visitors to the archipelago of volcanic islands and coral reefs will feel guilty if they so much as take time out to blink. Both Charles Darwin and Jacques Cousteau were impressed by the sheer diversity of colorful fish, surreally shaped coral, giant sea turtles, and rare marine birds that make their home in this live aquarium. December-March, when visibility is at its best, it's possible to see to depths of 20 meters (65 feet). Between July and November, an added bonus is watching the spectacle of humpback whales—16 meters (50 feet) in length and 40 tons in weight—who mate and give birth in the warm waters. September and October are the best months to see them in action. In July-August, rainy weather can result in excursions being canceled.

From Caravelas, it takes a little more than 2.5 hours to reach the Abrolhos archipelago by speedboat, and four hours by catamaran. Full-day excursions, with a minimum of 10 people, are offered by small operators, registered with the Instituto Chico Mendes environmental agency, such as Catamarã Horizonte Aberto (Av. das Palmeiras 313, tel. 73/3297-1474, www.horizonteaberto.com.br) and Catamarã Sanuk (Rua das Estrelas 80, tel. 73/3297-1344, www.abrolhos.net) for around R$350 per day. If you have time to spare (and money to spend), both companies also offer three-day overnight trips with accommodations and meals on schooners. Diving and snorkeling equipment can be rented for an extra fee. Advance reservations are advised. Beginners diving lessons are also available starting at R$150.

Accommodations and Food

In Caravelas, Pousada Liberdade (Av. Adalício Nogueira 1551, tel. 73/3297-2415, www.pousadaliberdade.com.br, R$170-200 d) is a low-key choice with bungalows sitting in a garden shaded by palm, mango, and cashew trees. More upscale and with a privileged beach location 7 kilometers (4.5 mi) from town is the Hotel Marina Porto Abrolhos (Rua da Baleia 333, Praia de Grauça, tel. 73/3674-1060, www.marinaportoabrolhos.com.br, R$190-275 d). The breezy, attractive guest rooms are in individual bungalows crowned by palm thatching and surrounded by plenty of swaying trees.

Carenagem (Rua das Palmeiras 210, tel. 73/3297-1280, 11:30am-11pm Mon.-Sat., R$25-35) is a lively restaurant/bar that serves up classic Bahian *moquecas* and unpretentious fish and meat dishes as well as live music.

Transportation and Services

For information about Caravelas and

Abrolhos, visit www.abrolhos.net. Águia Branca (tel. 71/4004-1010, www.aguiabranca.com.br) offers one daily direct bus to Caravelas from Salvador (15 hours, R$130) and three from Porto Seguro (4 hours, R$37) to the town of Teixeira de Freitas. From Teixeira de Freitas, O Brasileiro (tel. 73/3291-2529) operates five daily buses to Caravelas (2 hours, R$16). By car, turn off highway BR-101 at Teixeira de Freitas and continue along BA-290 for around 54 kilometers (33 mi) in the direction of the coastal town of Alcobaça. Head south for another 24 kilometers (15 mi) along the BA-001 to Caravelas.

Photo Credits

Title page: Igreja de Nosso senhor do Bonfim, Salvador © Embratur; pg 2: view of Pelurinho © Guillermo Avello/123RF; pg. 4 top: © Michael Sommers; bottom: © 123RF; pg. 5: © 123RF; pg. 12: © Michael Sommers; pg. 17: © 123RF; pg. 22: © Michael Sommers; pg. 23: © 123RF; pg. 38: © Michael Sommers; pg. 40: © Michael Sommers; pg. 47: © Michael Sommers; pg. 57: © Michael Sommers; pg. 72: © Michael Sommers

MAP SYMBOLS

═══ Expressway	○ City/Town	✈ Airport	⚓ Golf Course		
Primary Road	◉ State Capital	✈ Airfield	P Parking Area		
Secondary Road	✺ National Capital	▲ Mountain	▲ Archaeological Site		
Unpaved Road	★ Point of Interest	✚ Unique Natural Feature	⚲ Church		
Feature Trail	● Accommodation	Waterfall	Gas Station		
Other Trail	▼ Restaurant/Bar	⚑ Park	Glacier		
Ferry	■ Other Location	Trailhead	Mangrove		
Pedestrian Walkway	Δ Campground	Skiing Area	Reef		
Stairs			Swamp		

CONVERSION TABLES

°C = (°F - 32) / 1.8
°F = (°C x 1.8) + 32
1 inch = 2.54 centimeters (cm)
1 foot = 0.304 meters (m)
1 yard = 0.914 meters
1 mile = 1.6093 kilometers (km)
1 km = 0.6214 miles
1 fathom = 1.8288 m
1 chain = 20.1168 m
1 furlong = 201.168 m
1 acre = 0.4047 hectares
1 sq km = 100 hectares
1 sq mile = 2.59 square km
1 ounce = 28.35 grams
1 pound = 0.4536 kilograms
1 short ton = 0.90718 metric ton
1 short ton = 2,000 pounds
1 long ton = 1.016 metric tons
1 long ton = 2,240 pounds
1 metric ton = 1,000 kilograms
1 quart = 0.94635 liters
1 US gallon = 3.7854 liters
1 Imperial gallon = 4.5459 liters
1 nautical mile = 1.852 km

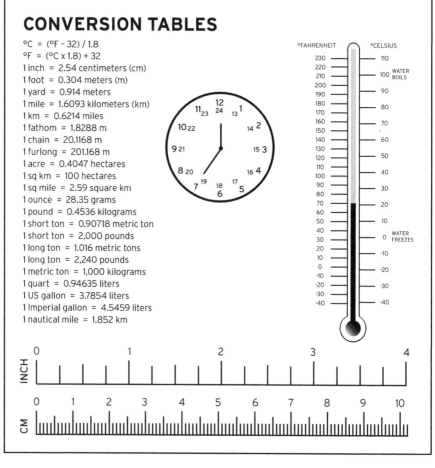

MOON SPOTLIGHT SALVADOR & BAHIA
Avalon Travel
a member of the Perseus Books Group
1700 Fourth Street
Berkeley, CA 94710, USA
www.moon.com

Editor: Sabrina Young
Series Manager: Kathryn Ettinger
Copy Editor: Kristie Reilley
Graphics and Production Coordinator:
    Lucie Ericksen
Map Editor: Kat Bennett
Cartographer: Stephanie Poulain

ISBN-13: 978-1-61238-940-0

Front cover photo: Iglesias Rosario Dos Pretos
in Pelourinho, Salvador © ostill | Dreamstime.
com

Printed in the United States

All recommendations, including those for sights,
activities, hotels, restaurants, and shops, are
based on each author's individual judgment.
We do not accept payment for inclusion in our
travel guides, and our authors don't accept
free goods or services in exchange for positive
coverage.

Although every effort was made to ensure
that the information was correct at the time of
going to press, the author and publisher do not
assume and hereby disclaim any liability to any
party for any loss or damage caused by errors,
omissions, or any potential travel disruption
due to labor or financial difficulty, whether
such errors or omissions result from negligence,
accident, or any other cause.

About the Author

Michael Sommers

© MICHAEL SOMMERS

Born in Texas and raised in Toronto, Michael Sommers grew up with travel on the brain — a consequence of time spent riding around in Oldsmobiles, Mini Mokes, and Pan Am jets in the company of a Gourmet-addicted mother and a father with a roving zoom lens.

When Michael turned 18 he took flight, setting down temporary roots in cities such as Bordeaux, Paris, Montreal, New York, and Lisbon. During this time, he earned a BA in Literature from McGill University and an MA in History and Civilizations from the École des Hautes Études en Sciences Sociales, where his thesis was "The Image of Brazil and Brazilians in Hollywood Cinema." He also worked as a writer and editor at magazines and newspapers and freelanced for publications such as *The New York Times, The International Herald Tribune,* and *The Globe and Mail.*

Michael first traveled to Brazil at the age of four. His only memory is being served a glistening orange wedge of papaya in the grand dining room at Rio de Janeiro's Hotel Gloria. Twenty years later, he returned to Brazil, where he was seduced by the intense, colorful landscapes, rich cultures, and warm people. Michael eventually settled down in Salvador, the baroque capital of Bahia, where he has worked as a writer and journalist for more than 15 years.

While Michael has yet to master the art of preparing *feijoada* (Brazil's national stew of beans, salted beef, and pork), he does make a mean *caipirinha.*

CPSIA information can be obtained at www.ICGtesting.com
Printed in the USA
LVOW01s1350020415

433025LV00004B/22/P

3 1901 05772 4025